SQUALL LINES

by Tim Dorsey

Selected Articles and Essays
Storm Surge Productions
Tampa, Florida

For Dennis
Best always!

Tim Dorsey

CONTENTS

NOVELS BY TIM DORSEY

For Tom Corcoran

INTRODUCTION

This book is the first collection of old articles that I've had published over the last thirty years.

It is not what you'd expect. But then nobody expected the Serge Storms series of novels.

People ask if Serge is my alter ego. No, he's my ego, straight up, except I have impulse control. Probably because I get to kill the people who piss me off in my novels. And get paid. The best of both worlds. Murder for hire, and you don't go to jail.

Now we have this book. Want insight into how Serge ticks? Track my writing evolution, from college through the present. People have described my style as the "brain-evacuation" school of prose. Fair enough. I've never been accused of being guarded. Or avoiding tangents, like the time I was five and running in circles with a jaw-breaker in my mouth, and suddenly I can't breathe and my mother is shaking me upside-down by the ankles, and I'm thinking, This is new. But that's just how I roll. Where was I?

Right, so here it all is to sort through. And I do mean sort. I was lying before: There actually are the parts you'd expect – crazed newspaper and magazine pieces in nascent Storms-esque rants. But there are also serious articles like a reflection on the crash of the Columbia. And quasi-academic (but highly useful) travel essays on how to find the best of tucked-away Florida. And, with a wince, I've reluctantly included some very early student newspaper and cub-reporter stabs at humor columns, if for no other reason to get them on the public record before the opposition. Think of these as archaeological research and make of them what you will. They're the writing equivalent of those "precious" photos your parents took of you eating spaghetti in a high chair with sauce all over face and noodles on top of your head.

But above all, keep in mind the price-point of this e-book. It's only $3.99, which means I threw in a bunch of bonus articles for nothing. So the writing in here you don't like: that's the free stuff.

I was going to say something else, but there's a squirrel outside my office window eating a potato chip.

Where was I?

Anyway, enjoy. Or not. It's only $3.99.

Tim Dorsey
Tampa, July 16, 2012

Carnet N. 170

Firma del Interesado

Vence: 23/5/86

JORGE ALBERTO ARGUELLO M.
Director Relaciones Públicas FF.AA.

MAXWELL AFB   1986   GUNTER AFS

PUBLIC AFFAIRS

OFFICIAL BUSINESS

TIM DORSEY is a recognized news media representative and is authorized access to the base. When this card is presented at the gate, Security Police are requested to contact the Public Affairs Office, 293-2018.

060

CHIEF OF PUBLIC AFFAIRS

PRESS

ALABAMA DEPARTMENT OF PUBLIC SAFETY

Date Issued: 9-27-82

The bearer TIM DORSEY is a duly authorized representative of THE AUBURN PLAINSMAN

Please extend to him every courtesy consistent with the public safety and the performance of your duties as outlined in Department of Public Safety guidelines.

NO. 1055   Director

PRESS PASS — POLICE AND FIRE LINES

POLICE DEPARTMENT
MONTGOMERY, ALA.

IDENTIFICATION CARD

Tim Dorsey
Name

Advertiser Journal
Representing

Signature

Chief of Police

C A P I T O L

PRESS

1 9 8 9

TIM C. DORSEY
Name

THE TAMPA TRIBUNE
Representing

MAXWELL AFB   1984   GUNTER AFS

PUBLIC AFFAIRS

OFFICIAL BUSINESS

Tim Dorsey is a recognized news media representative and is authorized access to the base. When this card is presented at the gate, Security Police are requested to contact the Public Affairs Office, 293-2018.

Alabama Journal
#47

DIRECTOR OF PUBLIC AFFAIRS

Part One

Midnight Writer

Tampa-Orlando, Florida 1993-2004

This section covers the transitional years from when I began working on my first novel until just after I started getting published. I was the night metro editor at the Tampa Tribune, *and after I got home in the wee hours, I'd split my time between working on* Florida Roadkill *and moonlighting under the pen name Sean Henry for the free-spirited Orlando Weekly newspaper. When* Roadkill *came out, I quit the* Trib *to hit the novels and the road full time.*

I was asked to examine the state of professional sports in Tampa, including a low-coveted new expansion team.

Blade Runners

(Orlando Weekly, 1994)

With the discovery of ancient human remains complicating its proposed downtown hockey arena, Tampa took another step toward that rarefied plateau in the sports world known as irrelevance.

The Bay area media, long desperate for a genuine athlete, decided the skeleton had more physical ability than most of the football team and gave him heavy coverage as the city's newest sports mascot, "Arena Man."

Meantime, the NBA returned Tampa's $100,000 franchise deposit check. Major League Baseball said not to think about a team for at least 10 years. The Tampa Bay Buccaneers, also, said not to think about a team for at least 10 years. And the Lightning continue to lose in St. Petersburg, where they moved from Tampa after declaring conditions unacceptable at an indoor livestock facility near Brandon.

And while the tiniest of Florida communities have mastered the management of spring training baseball, exhibition games in Tampa's hands are like a wind-blown pop fly in the sun. The Cincinnati Reds were lured away six years ago by economic dynamo Plant City. Current plans to attract the Yankees also are on the rocks, after officials -- God knows how -- got the deal hopelessly entangled with the construction of a new prison.

Tampa has seen all this and more before; it is a proud tradition. The USFL Bandits played fairly decently in a football-like league until creditors pawned their helmets. The Tampa Bay Rowdies soccer team collapsed under a collective yawn. Then Tampa's professional tennis team, The Action, disappeared while playing on a top-secret tour.

With shame no longer an issue, Tampa turned to made-up sports -- and promptly lost its arena football team, also to St. Petersburg. Commerce officials wisely downsized expectations, and the hunt was on. Professional lawn darts? A whiffle-ball franchise?

The non-planning paid off this year when Tampa was awarded one of 12 expansion roller hockey teams in the Roller Hockey International league.

In a slick brochure the league proclaims: "By 1997 there will be two roller hockey players to every ice hockey player." Similar statistics also show that by 1998, one out of every five people will be Elvis.

But season ticket prices for the Tampa Bay Tritons are no joke. Eleven home games in the "King Triton Throne" seats run $275 ($143 for "Triton Scepter" seats).

The Tritons know the challenge they face. And since the sport comes off like one of those beer ads (lawyer-rodeo, Sumo wrestler-high diving), they took the most important first step: They got a bitchin' logo. It shows some kind of mythological Greek god, possibly even Triton. Except that Triton, the son of Poseidon, had the tail of a fish and walked around blowing a conch-shell horn. Anyone acting like that in Tampa would trigger a hate crime. They have overcome this stigma by adding a scary mask and a spear-tipped hockey stick. Also, skates.

The Tritons kicked off their juggernaut May 21 with an open-house exhibition that included prizes, pizza and a special fans-skate-with-the-players hour (presumably more difficult for the Tritons than regular-season games).

Unfortunately, everything about the event said, "pretend there's ice."

The floor of the arena -- actually the Lightning's old home - was painted a rink-ice shade of light blue, and players dressed warm. Also, the only photo in the official brochure showed an ice hockey player (with skates cropped out), and ticket-buyers were enticed with a chance to attend the Stanley Cup playoffs. Fans even showed up in jerseys representing every NHL team.

Hanging over the whole event was some weird cross-pollination of business promotion on wheels. The Little Caesar's Pizza man ("pizza-pizza") skated around the concourse, as did young girls in skimpy sailor suits selling cruise-ship tickets. There were car dealer displays and stereo outlet tables and a giant hot-air balloon in front of the building.

All this activity on the edge of Interstate 4 drew people from three groups: ice hockey fans, Roller-blading fans, and people who thought it was a gun show.

Perhaps most surprising was the size of the roller hockey subculture. Two miniature rinks were set up behind the stands for a youth "clinic." But dozens of pre-schoolers in thousands of dollars' worth of gear seized control and launched a full-scale game, spinning and skating and handling sticks better than the adults. One kindergartner got checked over the wall and accidentally whacked a tiny girl hard in the side of the helmet with his stick; parents gasped, but the girl just turned and went swinging for the puck.

Outside the rinks, children constantly zoomed by in all directions until your nerves made you seek out a place to sit. Besides, the intrasquad Triton exhibition game was about to start, which could mean only one thing: really loud soul music on the PA system.

The Tritons did look sharp. They skated fast, shot accurately and made impressive saves. But because season tickets were on sale during the game, the object wasn't to score goals, but to crash into the glass as much as possible.

The Tritons have crashing into the glass down to a science. Crash into the glass when going for the puck. Crash into the glass when protecting the puck. Crash into the glass when you're standing alone and not getting enough attention.

It's a savvy marketing tactic. Nothing fools your senses into thinking you're at an actual hockey game more than watching people crash into the glass, except maybe boxing.

The Tritons open at home June 11, when they crash into the glass against Montreal. ESPN is scheduled to televise the playoffs of crashing into the glass in August.

Now the team just needs a good catch phrase for their radio spots. The Lightning sold a mountain range of tickets by burning into everyone's brain a cute, sing-song jingle that went, "Tam-pa Bay Light-ning -- Kick ice!"

Get it? Kick *ice*? Damn, that's funny.

So here's a suggestion for the new team. No need to thank us -- our satisfaction will be in your success. Ready?

"Tam-pa Bay Tri-tons -- Kick asphalt!"

During Clinton's first term, for reasons still unknown, Central Florida began experiencing a paranormal wave of 1970s nostalgia. I was asked to investigate.

The Return of the Leisure (Suit) Class

(Orlando Weekly, 1994)

Just as Jimmy Carter's popularity has crossed into positive territory now that he's out of office, the 1970s are rapidly becoming America's favorite ex-decade.

Consider the cabal of broadcast gurus, fashion nerds and the chronically lost who have begun strutting out a parade of saccharine memories on a bucks-for-blandness tour. Right on Soul-Train schedule, '70s music has invaded nightclubs, advertising jingles, movies and -- if you have FM in the car -- your head.

Makin' Love in My Chevy Van. The Night Chicago Died. Play That Funky Music, White Boy. That's the Way (Uh-huh Uh-huh) I Like It.

It's the same nostalgia phenomenon that's been cycling through most of the century. A yearning for one's high-school zeitgeist starts with an oldies song craze and ends with former teen idols on overnight-TV shilling Polident.

But the '70s are not some warm, fuzzy decade that puts its arm around your shoulder at the big reunion. It's not a lovable rebel in a leather jacket or a peacenik in a Grateful Dead tie-dye. No, this decade's nostalgia drags you into the bushes and forces itself on you. It's a walking Three Mile Island accident on platform shoes, festooned with pooka beads and WIN buttons.

Parents used to beckon kids back to their eras with forced-feedings of Sinatra, Elvis and the Beatles. But this time adults will be waving off their children with both arms. *We were there! Don't do it! It's devil-worship dance music!*

Which leads to only one thing: Disco Revival.

On a recent Tuesday night off Florida's Gulf Coast, a casino cruise ship hosted its new "Disco Night," sponsored by the nation's first all-'70s radio station -- Tampa Bay's Coast 107.3 FM. The ship's big-screen TV played NBC's national salute to the '70s, "The Beat is Back." (K.C. of The Sunshine Band was the one slightly heavier than Meatloaf.)

Spiro Agnew. The Mayaguez Incident. The Saturday Night Massacre. Idi Amin. Olga Korbut. Billy Beer.

Tom Frawley, a Coast station account manager, summed up the revisionist corporate view of 1970-1979: "A very positive era."

Anything else?

"Very positive."

But if the '70s has a maximum point-man in Florida, it is Coast's disc jockey/roving feel-good personality Scott Robbins, an unlikely and overqualified spokesman for the decade. In a smart blue blazer, tie and neat haircut, Robbins campaigns for the '70s like the ambassador of a non-aligned nation.

"An all-'70s station is really an oldies station of the future," Robbins says metaphysically. He predicts a long life for the format as the decade's children graze through the prime, 25- to 49-year-old demographic listening herd.

"Broadcasting in the '90s is narrow-casting," he says. "There are these niches, and now you're getting down to niches in eras."

But what about the reason that many people mention '70s music is only to say how much they hate it?

Robbins preaches that disco and other period music have a greater appeal than many are comfortable to admit. "I know there's a lot of peer pressure -- that it's really hip not to admit you like it.

"It all started in Comiskey Park," he says, referring to the infamous "Disco Demolition" promotion at a 1979 Chicago White Sox game. What began as a frolicking vinyl-record stomp turned into a full-bore riot as vicious bigotry against disco bubbled to the surface in a '70s version of a freedom-bus burning. The melee that spilled onto the field canceled the baseball game; more relevant, says Robbins, "It canceled disco."

Yet 15 years later, he anchors the morning slot and a Saturday night dance program, while a growing number of clubs across the state are regularly twirling the mirrored balls on '70s nights. As they say in the industry, disco is back with a bullet, and Robbins has a theory why: It's not rap.

Point, set and match to Robbins.

No, rap would not go over big on the cruise ship. But the given '70s theme still made for an odd night: a collision of nostalgia, gambling and maritime law. When a ship's officer walked by in his white uniform and cap, a young passenger cried out, "It's one of the Village People!"

Robbins sees the scene as a positive form of escapism and questions why the era should be faulted for that, when the sparks beneath the more highly touted '60s were social injustice and the Vietnam War.

And, in fact, Coast's playlist isn't all that frightening. Sure there's the occasional "Midnight at the Oasis," but there's also Creedence Clearwater Revival, The Doobie Brothers, and Free (that one good song).

Rather than protests, Robbins says his listeners tell him, "The '70s remind me of boys I used to go out with," "The '70s remind me of school," "The '70s remind me of the grungy clothes I used to wear."

Indeed, beneath its leisure suit and gold chain, the decade was -- if nothing else -- a safe place. It started with Roe vs. Wade and ended before AIDS. Marijuana was tolerated as a giddier form of alcohol before politicians decided there were votes to be made by lumping it in with crack. Even assassinations took a hiatus after the '68 slaughter of Bobby and Martin, resuming with the 1980 shooting of John Lennon. The exception was the attempt on George Wallace's life in 1972, but like all things '70s, it just mellowed him out.

Despite the music's chloroform haze, Hollywood entered a new golden era: "Patton," "M*A*S*H," "The Godfather," "Jaws," "The Sting," "Chinatown," "One Flew Over the Cuckoo's Nest," "Annie Hall," and the inspiration of "Rocky."

The '80s gave us "Rocky" sequels.

And a glance inside Webster's Third College Edition reveals the decade's contribution to verbal communication: "Boogie: verb intransitive, to dance to rock music." Booty, however, still has no recognized context.

Archie Bunker. Bobby Riggs. Legionnaire's Disease. G. Gordon Liddy. Son of Sam.

A dash of the '70s can be a tantalizing spice, as when the bloody film "Reservoir Dogs" threaded music from a mythical '70s radio festival through the body count. Hence, "Stuck in the Middle with You" by Stealers Wheel will now forever be linked with Michael Madsen's torture two-step.

But America's battle cry has never been Less is More, and the only good concept is one that has been thoroughly beaten to death. And that beating won't be pretty, with Sonny Bono-style second careers. The Bee Gees are already back, Mark Spitz has sent up a few semi-flat trial balloons, and chess-wizard-turned-nobody Bobby Fischer showed up in June in the middle of the Bosnian-Serbo-Croatian bloodbath to checkmate a flatulent Boris Spassky in a high-stakes game of Twister. Newspapers will dip into their morgues for the obligatory 20-year-anniversary filler stories. Prepare to get all soft and gooey about:

The oil embargo. Patty Hearst. Henry Kissinger. Hank Aaron's 715th home run. The Heimlich Maneuver.

So where does this leave the youth of today? The best place for answers is at their cultural brain stem, the mall. "Brady Bunch" T-shirts are being hawked on the concourse, the old A&W Root Beer drive-ins are now making a Chick-fil-A assault on the food court, and haircuts are reverting from chic mutilation to previously long.

Betsy, 22, sits in a courtesy booth under a sign that says "Information."

"Can I help you?" she asks.

"What do you know about the '70s?"

"I don't remember anything about the '70s," she says. "All I think of is bell-bottoms -- did they wear bell-bottoms then? -- and 'Saturday Night Fever' and the Bee Gees."

But it's veteran mall-shopper and recent journalism graduate Christy, 23, who puts things in perspective: "Who's George Wallace?"

Donnie and Marie. Laverne and Shirley. Woodward and Bernstein. Mork and Mindy.

At Barbarella in downtown Orlando, 26-year-old Alex Dellagatta spins the classics each week on Mondays' "Bad Disco Night."

Younger people who don't remember '70s music from the first go-'round "seem to be very receptive to it," he says. "They realize that music they listen to on the radio is nothing but remixes from the disco era."

Orlando's own WMMO-98.9 FM hosts a "Lost '70s" request program.

"We've been doing it since before the '70s were actually hot," says promotion director Jim Stout. "A lot of our program is based on '70s music that you don't hear on typical radio stations -- Peter Frampton, Ozark Mountain Daredevils, Orleans. Everyone can remember where they were when these '70s acts were at their peak; everyone has a story to tell."

But there's the dark side: "I can't believe I wore clothes like that," says Stout. "I didn't know it was corny until I grew older and looked back."

Besides evoking memories of mood rings and lava lamps, WMMO brings the '70s back in the flesh in its lunchtime concert series at Church Street Station. The likes of Melanie, Sugarloaf, Dr. Hook, Wet Willie -- just this past week, it was Jefferson Starship -- perform their own brand of '70s rebellion for the bologna-sandwich set.

Over in Tampa, the Ybor City district is stacking its chips on '70s fashion, from the Blue Funk boutique (where "Charlie's Angels" T-shirts sell for $17 next to $50 corduroy overalls) to Uptown Threads ("The time was then ... the look is NOW!"). Says Bil at Uptown: "We can't keep platform shoes in stock."

He adds, "Last year a lot of alternative people were into the '70s, and now it's mainstream. ... Now you've got a lot of people with black in their closet next to bell-bottoms, next to grunge."

But Bil himself, at 35, has much dimmer memories. "It was kind of lost really; there was no vision. ... And now you look back and there's a real campiness to it, and maybe that's what appeals to the high-school set -- campy and not serious.

"I don't think anyone respects it. It's the Rodney Dangerfield of decades."

But if the boutiques and clubs spoon-feed nostalgia, Retro Records in Orlando fist-shoves the '70s down your throat. If you can remember it, they have it in spades at 59 N. Bumby Ave.

Cher's Makeup Center, $75; "Welcome Back Kotter" album box, $35; "Dukes of Hazzard" lunch box, $25; Susan Dey (of "Partridge Family LAW") paper dolls, $15; and the redundant Andy Gibb wastebasket, $40.

Retro's Vedat Gulen said much '70s memorabilia is big with the kids, especially debris from the band KISS.

"There's KISS record players, AM radios, alarm clocks. ... (The kids) used to come in and ask, 'Is that a new thing they just released?'"

His reaction to teens' fascination with the Me Decade? "It kind of makes me snicker a little, actually."

And now we've reached the cultural equivalent of an ugly couple having children: the '90s-ization of the '70s. Madonna is doing disco schtick on tour, and Disney World has genetically engineered a corporately policed strain of nostalgia at its '70s dance club on Pleasure Island, 8TRAX.

On Kissimmee's own Vegas strip, U.S. 192, the shingle hanging on the Wound 'N Around store boasts: "50s, '60s, '70s Nostalgic gifts." But salesman Eric Lariviere -- standing inside a '62 Chevy Impala/sales counter -- says they haven't gotten the '70s in just yet.

"We just put '70s up (on the sign) so we could throw it in if we wanted," he says. "It leaves the door open for the future."

As Christy from the mall thoughtfully summed up: "I don't care."

Road Warrior

(Tampa Tribune, 1999)

TAMPA -- They're not supposed to have hecklers at book signings, are they?

That was the question in my road-weary head twelve days after quitting my job at the Tampa Tribune and standing before an audience in a South Florida book store. I was pitching my dark humor first novel, "Florida Roadkill," a satirical love affair with my home state.

The older woman with the thick European accent in the front row did not grasp satire. She also did not grasp book signings. She seemed part of that population segment that joins an audience at the Strawberry Festival for the demonstration of a new twin-turbine kitchen frappe machine, thinking only: There are a bunch of Samsonite chairs set up -- I must sit in one.

First, she turned on another member of the audience, then she attacked me relentlessly. We didn't appreciate Florida enough and we were lazy and her medicine cost too much. I tried to recognize another member of the audience, but the book-signing bomber wouldn't stop talking. I tried saying her points were on target, so she disagreed with me agreeing with her.

It was a no-win -- you can't return fire on a little old lady. I was stunned silent. This can't be happening, I thought, I've just quit my job. I began feeling faint; objects started to glow. I looked down at the microphone in my hand and felt like I was holding an embarrassing honeymoon accessory in front of everyone.

The bookstore's host came to my rescue by clapping her hands sharply and saying, "That concludes our talk, please line up for autographs." But by then the audience was so painfully uncomfortable that several briskly left the store.

It wasn't what I expected. Actually, I had no idea what to expect when my New York publisher, HarperCollins, pitched their idea. To tie in with the road theme of the book, they wanted me to trace the outline of the state of Florida, starting in Jacksonville and taking only old coastal routes on a marathon roadtrip. And I wasn't just supposed to go to bookstores. They wanted me to stop at all kinds of crazy, kitschy old Florida roadside attractions, taking pictures with a digital camera. They wanted me to use a laptop and upload the photos and daily travelogue to the Internet each night from my motel room. They would give me magnetic car door signs like electricians and plumbers (I would later stick one of the signs on an Apollo capsule at Kennedy Space Center for a quick photo before NASA security detected me).

Would I do it, they asked tentatively.

Are you kidding? That's a dream job description!

I hit the road like a rock star, starting in Atlantic Beach and heading down A1A. One week later, I felt more like Boxcar Willie -- exhausted, confused, unregular -- limping in on fumes to the ambush by the Condo Commando woman in the front row.

That was almost three months ago, and I'm happy to say things have improved. The facts: 52 bookstores in 75 days, 2,300 books signed, 4,000 miles on a '92 Chrysler. Six pounds gained, then eight lost. Dozens of new friends.

Despite the body/brain toll, it has been a wonderful megadose of Florida, making me love the state more. You can live here your whole life, but you'll never know this place the way you will if you're forced to race through 23 nights in different motels, down a compressed succession of beach towns, watching terrain and culture change in time-lapse photograpy: the First Coast, the Space Coast, the Treasure Coast, the Gold Coast, the Nature Coast ... No reasonable person would ever vacation this way, just like they wouldn't drink orange juice concentrate without mixing with water.

I climbed the St. Augustine lighthouse and the Castillo de San Marcos. I visited Marineland, the Daytona Speedway, the Boardwalk, Boot Hill Saloon and the Launch Pad Bar. I saw dolphins, Stiltsville, Cape Florida, art deco hotels. I washed clothes with migrants in a laundromat while listening to a pre-recorded interview of myself on local radio. I raced an SEC locomotive along Old Dixie Highway. I got caught in the middle of a domestic altercation in the parking lot of an economy hotel at 1 a.m., a police chase in Fort Lauderdale, and a chic South Beach dance floor.

It happens so fast, you're just reacting the whole time, and you can really only digest it in retrospect. When I first set out, crowds were tiny. The book had just gone on sale and there hadn't been much press coverage. Then the work of the publicity people in New York started paying off. Feature articles and reviews began appearing in the cities ahead of me. I was finally getting air cover: media carpet bombing softening up the beaches before I stumbled ashore.

More people came out, more books signed. The pace picked up. I kept getting e-mail on the fly, scheduling new interviews, rescheduling old ones. I was forced to do what I swore I never would -- I started talking on a cell phone in the car. More e-mail, scraps of mind-bending info passed along matter-of-factly: The first printing ran out 10 days into the tour and they went back to press for a second printing; the *New York Times* was doing a review; back to press again for a third printing; the London publisher was sponsoring some kind of contest to promote the book. First prize: trip to Florida.

Half-way through a four-day stand in Miami, my body said: no more grease! I filled a cooler with romaine hearts and carrots. In Naples, my mind said, I'm gonna tear my eyes out if I have to eat any more of this damn rabbit food. When I ran low on energy, I'd stop for a king-size 7-Eleven coffee with three sugars and four of those little lavender amaretto creamers; I'd add ice and chug the whole thing at the cash register, and now I was ready to pull back onto U.S. 1 without my car.

Then a breakthrough. I went to change into my dress clothes before a book signing one evening in Naples. I was sweating a lot during this period and would change at the last minute, doing a Superman-style wardrobe switch in a gas station restroom. This particular night, I had one clean shirt left. I dropped it in the toilet. I stared silent and helpless into the bowl and thought: You have sinned and God is punishing you.

I walked into the bookstore in a wrinkled Hawaiian shirt that I'd purchased as a goof on the strip in Fort Lauderdale. I matched the shirt with cargo shorts and flip-flops. Then I crept into the store, ready to explain the mishap and apologize for my appearance. But the bookstore people were already laughing in approval. It was an ice-breaker with the audience, too. Everyone thought it was a brilliant, intentional tie-in with the book. What had once been a hapless personal life was now lucrative shtick.

I began getting a bunch of e-mail from people at previous book signings, who were tracking my movements on the Web, suggesting places to go, telling me what to watch out for, rooting me on like I was Cool Hand Luke eating boiled eggs.

And all along the way I started to notice something bigger and better. A while before the tour, my agent and editor had said they thought Florida fiction might have already played itself out and gone into decline. But I saw something much different in my travels. Carl Hiaasen, James Hall, Edna Buchanan, Elmore Leonard et al. hadn't saturated the market; they'd just whetted appetites. All these people showing up at the stores, all these new friends weren't into some sub-genre. They were into Florida. A new heritage movement. And being such a young state, they were ready to lap up anything they could find. The events became more like a string of meetings for a secret society that was going public, and it was heartening to see there were so many of us. Yes, give us books about the psychotic behavior and peripheral weirdness we see all around every day -- and we will laugh in its face. We are a proud people.

We are Floridians.

Sea to Shining Sea

(Various publications, 2004)

Confession time: Before the book tours, I was an ill-traveled Florida hick. So for me, the tours have been an unexpected journey of personal growth, finally discovering my own country, every corner of America from a Woody Guthrie song.

And it is indeed a big country, amazingly rugged and diverse. From canyons to prairies to snow-capped peaks. Farmers, rappers, immigrants, descendants of the Mayflower. And through it all, a single over-arching lesson about humanity was hammered home again and again. No matter how different people are, it does mean you can't make fun of them.

Here's my report:

Pittsburgh -- Never been here before. Boy, can these people talk! Here are the parts I remember: The city has more bridges that any other place in the world. Mr. Rogers is from here. They don't make much steel anymore. A recent mayor wanted to paint the bridges pink and cadmium yellow until calmer heads prevailed.

Washington D.C. – Took the wrong exit, got lost and circled the Pentagon a couple of times at midnight and am now on some kind of list. Someone's getting rich off concrete barricades. Finally found my hotel on embassy row next to the consulate for Micronesia. Why is it there? What can't they handle by e-mail?

Baltimore -- A city that appears to be made up entirely of the bad parts of town.

Boston – Talk about your airport security! There's a giant sign with the color-coded alert (today: panic-level kiwi). To avoid accusations of profiling, they *over*-profile. Every elderly Japanese woman is pulled out of line so they don't hurt the feelings of the guys in the bomb-shaped shoes.

San Diego – Lots of caution signs along the interstate that have silhouettes of fleeing families, which are warnings to avoid running over illegal Mexicans or the Von Trapp family. The silhouettes show the family members, in descending height, running hand-in-hand across the highway. This is true: the last little girl at the end of the family silhouette is actually flying with her feet off the ground. Details are the key to appreciating a new place.

Houston -- This was the first city where I decided to rent a car and drive myself around. I did the signing, turned in the Hertz and made it to George Bush International Airport with an hour and a half to spare, feeling pretty good about myself for saving money on a chauffeur. I went to the counter and asked where my boarding gate was.

"At the other airport."

New York -- Honed my pedestrian survival skills by watching the natives. Ignore the "Walk / Don't Walk" signals and instead think of it all as a National Geographic herd of hunted gazelles dashing between watering holes. Later, I nearly bonked heads with Tipper Gore when we leaned over from opposite sides of a table to sign the same publicity poster in the greenroom of a booksellers' convention. I thought, if that's Tipper, Al shouldn't be far behind. And there he was just to my right. I decided not to mention I was from Florida.

Seattle -- Climate whiplash from Phoenix. But a fabulous city. Boeing, Space Needle, original Starbucks. I don't think there's anything else, except I could be wrong because I was in a cloud the whole time. Very civilized, like Scandinavia or National Public Radio. The book signing was downtown, so I walked, using my newly acquired New York pedestrian skill-set. Then I noticed I was all alone in the middle of the street. No cars coming, all the other people standing ten deep, still, on each corner, staring at me in horror like I had a bloody ax. They told me at the book store that jaywalking is about a hundred dollars.

Portland – Chose to rent a car again and drive myself down from Seattle to enjoy the Pacific Northwest. Learned it's against the law to pump your own gas in Oregon. Except if you don't know this, it's the beginning of a very interesting conversation: "Excuse me, what are you doing?" "Pumping gas in my rental car." "But you can't." "Sure I can, it's easy." "Give me that." "Let go of the handle." "You let go." Portland is creepy.

Cleveland -- Spent most of my time on the runway in a blizzard while they de-iced a long line of aircraft. And this is what I learned about Cleveland: De-icing is a fascinating process when it's someone else's plane.

Phoenix -- I never get jet lag. I experience climate lag. It was 106 degrees by the time we hit the Phoenix Barnes & Noble. But they kept saying it was a dry heat. Here's the advantage of dry heat: You don't get clammy *as you die*. Didn't notice a big homeless problem here.

Los Angeles -- Never been before. I asked the chauffeur to point out the Hollywood sign when we got near. Zipped all over three counties, saw everything as it blurred by the window. Burbank, Beverly Hills, Pasadena. No Hollywood sign. Autographed some books on the Sunset Strip four doors down from the Viper Room. It began getting dark, and we headed back to LAX.

"There's the Hollywood sign!" I snapped a picture.

"No, that's a Hollywood Video."

San Francisco -- California is the over-protective parents that home school and make their kids wear helmets in the bathtub. My hotel room had something in it called an ionizer. It was plugged into the wall and hummed and was supposed to make me live longer. The hallway outside had big signs that said the state required them to be posted and notify guests that the hotel was constructed solely from materials that can kill me. I phoned the front desk for another ionizer.

Indianapolis – Didn't stop here. Looks small from the air.

Denver -- My driver really pushed the bottled water on me. She said I needed it to fend of altitude sickness, which has a way of creeping up. By the time I noticed any symptoms, it would too late.

"What do you mean? I'll die?"

"No, but you won't like it."

We hit a Borders and I felt a bit light-headed. The people I was talking to at the info desk began glowing and I grabbed the edge of the counter so I wouldn't wack my chin in case my legs went. I wobbled back to the car and tanked up on the water. When I felt better, we headed to another book signing. They had the cover of my book meticulously reproduced in the frosting of a cake. They said they had ordered it from a pornographic cake store.

New Orleans -- Everyone was drunk.

Dallas – The folks in this city seemed very nice. I was only there for a flight connection, so I only saw the airport. And I didn't see most of that. But the people I met at my gate from Nebraska and Delaware were quite pleasant. I've decided I like Dallas.

Tampa – Ah, the book tour is over, and I'm finally heading home. I've splurged for an upgrade to first class. My brain can barely function from exhaustion, but my job is done. Just relax and enjoy the flight. The pilot comes on the intercom and says the temperature in Chicago is twenty-nine, which is interesting because I don't live there.

Hooray for Hollywood

(Sarasota Magazine, 2003)

I couldn't even act dignified. I was riding around Los Angeles in the back of cab, fidgeting with radioactive excitement, snapping a million photos out the window like a tourist-fool, click, click, click, experiencing the proverbial urge to stop and pinch myself.

This is why: Hollywood had just sent for me.

My fifth Florida novel was hitting the book stores, and the movie rights had just been sold. The powers that be had flown out to L.A. for several books signings and to "take meetings" with movie people. I had spent fifteen years in the newspaper business and had *gone* to lots of meetings. This was the first time I'd be *taking* them. They told me this was good. Everything was paid for. People were nice to me.

Something was very wrong.

I had the sensation that a big, cartoon cane was about to reach out from off-stage, snag me around the neck -- "Okay, you imposter, let's go" -- and yank me out of this dream. So that's what my camera was for. I wanted a photographic record of this trip before this massive intellectual fraud was discovered. Then someday I could sit in a rocking chair and show my grandchildren, "This here was back in '03 when I took meetings." ... Click, click, click.

I arrived at my movie agent's suite in a high-rise on the Sunset Strip. The tower held offices of all kinds of famous film people like Toby McGuire. The receptionist told me the names of some of the other celebrities, but I don't remember because I was tingly the whole time. I just sat in the lobby smiling up at all the autographed movie posters on the wall. Clint Eastwood didn't smile back.

The receptionist said I could go in. The agent came out from around his desk, extending a hand to shake.

"You wore a suit?"

I smile and nod. What did that mean?

"You're the writer," he added. "You could have worn anything. Writers are expected to be eccentric. They can dress down and wear grunge if they want. That's what the directors do. Directors are the worst-dressed people in this town. Especially the female directors. They want respect, so they dress as bad as possible on purpose -- baggy stuff, no makeup -- to identify with the crew. But you're the writer; you could have worn anything, and the fact that you still wore a suit says even more."

I smile and nod.

"Let's go to lunch."

We eat at a Beverly Hills hamburger joint with tassled menus and giant red leather chairs and prices like it took the whole cow to make one burger. He tells me that anything about Florida is white-hot right now with "The Suits." But that could change quickly. And then it could change back. He said my timing was perfect either way. He explains the deal they've put together for me, with about a gazillion contingencies that kick in for overseas distribution and sequels and spinoffs and action figures and if there's a total lunar eclipse in Paraguay.

We get back to the office. He checks his watch and stops at the receptionist's desk. "Get Tim a cab. They're expecting him at the studio in thirty minutes."

He turns to me. "It's important that you sell yourself to these people. But you're the writer, so you really don't have to sell yourself."

I smile and nod.

He shakes my hand. "You'll do great."

The cab whisks me across town. I get out my camera. Click, click, click.

Suddenly, I'm at the studio. I'm in an elevator. I'm sitting in a suite on the fourth floor. I'm on a long, plush couch. Two executives are facing me in chairs at least fifteen feet away, nothing between us but an expanse of carpet. One is in a suit, like an accountant. The other is in a T-shirt and looks like he just came from the gym. Behind them, the whole wall is a giant, tinted plate-glass window overlooking the Hollywood sign. I'm getting woozy.

The executives lean forward, not saying anything, smiling at me with zealous anticipation as if I'm going to do something incredible like pull twenty ping-pong balls out of my mouth. I don't. They glance at each other begin laughing.

I smile and nod.

They start telling jokes about Florida and laughing and leaning toward me even more, to see if I laugh. I do. That makes them laugh. The meeting's over.

Back to the hotel. I take a shower. The phone's ringing when I get out.

It's my agent. "Just talked to the studio. Heard the meeting went well. They said you were funny."

I head down the stairs. Two young producers are waiting for me in the hotel lobby. They're the ones who discovered the books a couple of years ago and got the whole ball rolling. We're going to dinner. I climb in their car and we head up the Sunset Strip, past Chateau Marmont where John Belushi bought it, to a chic bistro with a mechanical bull. The producers string together words in ways I've never heard, like, "I've got to stop dating actresses. They're all neurotic." They tell me I ought to stop in and check out SkyBar, up at the Mondrain, where the big stars hang.

I tell them I heard it's almost impossible to get in.

They said it was, except the trick is "to go with a super model."

I smile. "Where am I going to find a super model?"

They start laughing. They said they heard I was funny. The mechanical bull sends a super model flying behind me.

The next morning: rise and shine, book signing day. I'm met in the hotel lobby by my "media escort." The escorts are local liaisons who know everyone in the publishing biz and make sure you get everywhere you need to be, get everything you want. We head toward Santa Monica. He looks familiar. He tells me he used to play Douglas Brackman's low-life brother in a three-episode arc on *L.A. Law.* He tells me stories about his friend Joe Pantoliano from *The Sopranos* as we arrive at a nearby Borders, where the store rep played the wife of an FBI agent in a made-for-TV movie starring Michael Gross and David Soul. I ask another store rep if L.A. is always like this. He says not everyone is an actor, but all the cab drivers have screenplays under their seats, just in case.

L.A. book signing are the opposite of studio meetings. While the writer is king among the producers, actors rule the book stores. I walk past a pile of books that were signed by the person just before me. Mariel Hemingway. My escort says stores have actor signings all the time, three or four a week. I shake hands with the manager. He's polite, but I can tell. Next to Mariel Hemingway, I'm like some guy who just farted.

We drop by more stores in Pasadena, Orange County, Venice Beach ("Fred Ward was just in. You know, Gus Grissom from *The Right Stuff*?"). We're leaving and something catches my eye. I stare at a street loon standing perfectly still in the middle of the road with a plastic trash bag over his head.

The escort chuckles. "You find that strange?"

"No," I say. "Finally something that reminds me of Florida."

Reading in Jacksonville, 2001

Part Two

College Years
Auburn University 1979-1983

I joined the student newspaper, the Plainsman, at the beginning of my freshman year. It was my first experience getting published. It was also my first exposure to the Deep South. I felt like a Martian dropped into Alabama. So did Alabama. By my senior year, I was the editor. I figured it was some kind of cosmic joke. So did Alabama.

The Student Life

Do any of you remember getting something in the mail from the government a while ago that said "Important Document"? I think it was called a W-2 form. Anyway, I was just curious because I threw mine out. The way I see it, any country that allows someone like me to live alone, unsupervised, deserves whatever it gets.

A country has to be tough as nails to leave me to my own devices. The possibilities even scare me, but my government remains calm. They know how to deal with people like me. They send us to college.

For us young Americans too immature for the real world, college gives us four years to screw-up before it starts counting. If you screw-up too much during this time, you become eligible for a two or four year extension known as "graduate school." If you never stop screwing-up, you become a teacher.

Among the things we're supposed to get a handle on at college are cooking, washing, dressing, landlords, utilities, the phone company, a checking account and personal odors. Let's take a brief look at my scorecard and see how I'm doing. My diet is my weakest area. I come from the "Take No Prisoners" school of cooking, which means that all dials on the stove and oven are considered "on/off" switches. Crank 'em all the way left or right. I don't use the timer because I have a smoke detector.

I have troubles with landlords. Whenever landlords inspect my apartment before returning my deposit, they always say picky things like, "Wasn't there a wall here?" But I've found a way to deal with these troublesome people. When you visit their office and you give notice you'll be leaving at the end of the month, casually light an entire book of matches one by one and watch them burn. When the book is empty, laugh insanely. This ensures an early deposit return and free moving-out assistance.

As far as clothing is concerned, I practice what is known as the super-time-efficient (and get-to-class-on-time) practice of "approximate dressing." In approximate dressing, there are only two types of sock. White and dark. All white socks match. All darks match. And in approximate dressing, clothes only must match by species. For examples, "pants" go with "shirts." To master approximate dressing, you must look like you've dressed in the dark.

I wash my clothes on a rotational basis. Apparel is divided in two categories: clothes piled up on the floor, and clothes in another pile on the floor. The first pile is in the "wear" cycle. So is the second. Washing could occur at any time.

Personal odors are more of a paranoia than a problem, but this is not an area to gamble with. My game plan is to wear sweaters as much as possible, which not only covers up unironed shirts, but act as giant odor eaters.

I have a kitchen table covered with bills. It might just be me, but it seems they're sending more and more literature with bills these days. Here's a pamphlet on saving energy. Here's one on helping the handicapped and another on why rates are going up again and it's not their fault. All very nice, but how much do I owe? South Central Bell occasionally sends me recipes. This month's recipe is "Black Cherry Garden Salad." It begins, "George Washington might have spared his father's cherry tree if he tasted this black cherry treat." Remember now, this is a phone bill.

My gas bill isn't any different. Here's a little booklet they sent me entitled "Cold Weather Equals Higher Gas Bills." I feel like sending it back and saying, "I'm sorry … I believe you meant to mail this to the brain-dead." Along with this valuable booklet is my computer card with a lot of numbers on it. One of them is 32642329100055793. What in the hell kind of number is this? Certainly not the kind I want to see when I open a bill.

At the bottom of the card it says, "Keep this portion for your records." This lets us know what part of the bill to throw out.

All of this goes right into the trash. I don't have the time to sift through all their propaganda and cooking tips to figure out what I owe. I'll just wait until they're ready to get serious and make things easy for me. Sure enough, three weeks later I get another bill. No dumb pamphlets or stupid recipes. Just one envelope. One card. One number in red. "Disconnect Notice." Now this is a bill. I'm ready to pay.

But I always make the mistake of paying by check. My checking account is an unexplained phenomenon. Every week, another Andrew Jackson is sucked into the black hole of bad checks.

I do not understand my bank. It remains a mystery to me. However, I have a theory. I believe that my bank is actually two banks. Both banks occupy the same building at the same time and use the same name. This could be the only answer because both banks treat me so differently. One bank says, "How are you today?" and gives me a toaster. The other keeps me under surveillance with cameras. One bank is open when I'm in class. The other bank is closed when I want my money. One bank offers me the advantage of a "high"-yield savings account as a prestige customer. The other chains their pens to the foundation.

But my bank is nothing compared to the phone company, even when I visit their showroom for something as simple as ordering a phone to start being their customer.

"I would like a black desk phone."

"Would you like a trimline or maybe a touch-tone?" asks the clerk.

"No, thank you. Just a black desk phone."

"How about our princess phone or our Americana eagle. We have Mickey Mouse and Pac-Man and one shaped like footballs. We even have a phone in the likeness of Bear Bryant if that's what you like."

"That's not what I want. I want a black desk phone."

"What color would you like that in?"

"Black, please!"

"You don't have to get angry. Just pick out the one you want." She gestures to several tables displaying myriad weird objects, none of which look like a phone. I look for a while, but I only see airplanes, race cars and Snoopy. No phones. Finally, I spot a black desk phone in the corner.

"I'll take that one," I say.

"I'm sorry," she replies. "That's not a phone. It's a cigarette lighter that looks like a phone."

I just enrolled in graduate school.

I can't get away from the guy

I get fooled constantly by the same guy. He's my ego; he's very convincing.

I know another guy. He's my perception. He wants me to see things the way they are so I can know truth. My ego is a cruising battleship. My perception is the size of a pea.

Perception will be telling me how insignificant I am in the scheme of the cosmos. Just then my ego will stumble in, drunk on self-deception, and begin raving. "No! You're a big deal! Demand special treatment!"

My perception wants me to feel good about my lot in life. "You're one of the luckiest people on earth. You should never be unhappy. You could have been born a bug!" But then my ego: "Your problems are many. You are alone and no one understands. You deserve More! More! More!"

Whenever I've just had an argument, my perception says, "Forget about it. It's not worth it." But my ego will carry on for hours. "I've got it! The perfect comeback! Why didn't I think of it when that guy was being such a jerk? I really hate him. He has so many faults, too. Let's list them, shall we?" Egos waste a lot of time.

There are a lot of egos out there these days. Egos ride in sports cars with the windows down and the radio on full blast so three city blocks can share their superior taste in music. Egos sit in the stands at football games and let everyone know they could call better plays than the coach. Egos talk loudly in restaurants and laugh at their own jokes. This is to announce that anyone not dining with them is settling for a great deal less than what life has to offer.

Egos have a cool image. They wear mirror sunglasses and T-shirts that say, "I'm a wild and crazy guy." Egos drink too much and put on party hats. My ego hates other egos. Being held hostage by your ego is nothing to be ashamed of. Egos are muscular and have hairy arms. Most mornings my ego pulls me out of bed by the collar: "Go out today and believe you are not the same as others." I usually just hand over Perception without a struggle.

Egos give each of us a moral code based on what's best for our interests at any particular time. We all do this. We'll be trying to cross the street: "These damn drivers! They never stop at the crosswalks! They think they own the road!" Ten minutes later we're driving on the same street, "Look at these damn pedestrians! Just puttering along in the crosswalk like I have all the time in the day!"

This kind of "my-group-correctness" can be a lot of fun, like when we're rooting for our football team. God himself has ordained the Tigers to smite our enemies at Alabama, Georgia and any other rat-hole they may come from on our way to the national championship that we, the chosen people, so richly deserve. Of course, the students at Alabama and Georgia think the same way, but they're wrong.

Our egos would be very sad without someone to call incorrect.

A few people are going to be pretty shook when we get to heaven, and we're just a bunch of souls floating around like glowing ping-pong balls. "Hey, God! Where are the blacks? And the Jews? And the rednecks? We can't tell 'em apart! How are we gonna feel superior? ... What? We're all the same? You just disguised us? ... It was Your idea of situation comedy?"

Some groups are so alike that it's scary, but egos must find differences. Liberals and conservatives are hilarious. Conservatives hate Communists. Liberals hate Communists too, but are nice to them to irritate the conservatives. And the conservatives don't hate minorities half as much as they hate liberals: "Just because I'm white, it doesn't mean I owe you anything," a middle-class, white conservative will tell a middle-class, white liberal. A few minutes later the liberal will be will be pointing out the only black guy at the party. "Uh, the gentleman over there in the green shirt."

Blacks also act curiously. They have a group called the NAACP. Here's a group that's for the advancement of African-Americans, but still calls them colored people. Must be a white guy running it.

Prejudice is a serious thing. Even I am persecuted for the color of my skin. Some bigots came up to me the other day. "Tim, where's your tan? Don't you get any rays? Stand back snowman, you're blinding me!"

What a shock. My own people.

Thinking about this stuff is perception. Printing it in a newspaper for everyone to read is ego.

In the early 1980s, the Auburn University faculty and administration were in the midst of a civil war so severe it drew a full-page report from Time *magazine, which concluded with an editorial quote from the student paper pleading with the president to resign. I don't think he was happy with me. In any case, columns such as this simultaneously fanned the flames and lightened the mood. There's a lot of inside-baseball references, but you get the picture.*

Auburn's New Clothes

If no one else is going to admit it, then I will. I do not understand the liberal arts/land-grant conflict. Sure, I said I understood it. I even wrote editorials about it and explained academic nuances to reporters from the *Atlanta Constitution* and *Columbus Enquirer* who wanted to know "What the hell's going on at Auburn?"

I was bluffing.

As the crisis exploded in our faces like a trick cigar, I scrambled to stay informed, but it was all too much. So I did what everyone else was doing. I repeated the "informed language" like a trained parakeet. Informed language consists of all the key phrases to use when you seek to appear informed but have no idea what you're talking about.

"You want to know what's going on at AU? I'll tell you: Our land grant heritage is conflicting with the liberal arts progression toward the comprehensive university concept."

"But what does that mean?"

"The president and the faculty hate each other's guts."

I wanted to know what the issues really were, but nobody would stop using informed language and utter something substantial. We had a classic case of the emperor's new clothes. Everyone *said* they understood what was going on. But nobody dared ask any questions because they would become uninformed and thus not allowed to hate anyone.

But the truth of the liberal arts/land-grant conflict is far simpler than anyone suspects. The two groups just don't relate to each other. Many reasons have been given: One group is rural, the other urban. One group likes the way things are. The other asks too many questions. But whenever two groups don't relate, there is only one real reason.

They don't party the same.

Republicans and Democrats. Blacks and whites. Greeks and independents. You and any group you don't dig. The difference is the partying.

There was bound to be a conflict at Auburn. Dr. Funderburk just doesn't party like Dr. Bond. Funderburk serves bourbon and watches "Gunsmoke." Bond has strobe lights and inflatable women. It was the classic partying conflict. Only one thing was missing: a sophisticated reason to hate the other group. Enter stage right: land-grant philosophy. Stage left: liberal arts philosophy.

The two camps divvied everything. Land grant annexed Engineering, Agriculture and Pharmacy. Liberal arts seized Business and Architecture and Fine Arts. Land grant took the beer and pretzels. Liberal arts grabbed the wine and cheese. Land grant bought some Skoal. Liberal arts scored Colombian. The party was on.

Once we see it like this, we can begin to understand what "informed language" is really telling us. For instance, "political ties" is a term thrown around a lot. What ties? Where? Ah, but this is not the issue.

The issue is that political ties are bad, and we are against them. "Vested interests" is another big one. These are campaign contributors. To the liberal artists, "Farm Bureau" is not an insurance company; it is the amorphous, unseen entity of the darkest forces in the universe. "Certain elements on the Board of Trustees" means "that jerk Bamberg."

If land-granters say "History Department," this means "scum." "Arts and Sciences" is a multi-purpose term for all that is against what football stands for. "That gang up-state" is the code-name for all the stuff we know in our hearts is going on, but just can't prove.

The word "faculty" has lots of extra meaning. "Pointy heads" and "Commie lovers" for starters. A "liberal" is even worse. This is a Commie-lover from out-of-state. Sometimes people go for air-raid-siren words like "humanist." This is Joe McCarthy language for "atheist."

"The library" represents reading and everything un-American that it leads to. "In the best interest of Auburn University" is coward-talk for "We do it my way or I'm going home with my toys."

And finally, the "liberal arts/land-grant conflict" translates to "I don't like them. They don't party right."

With the university civil war heating up at the end of '82, the administration and faculty began issuing a regular series of competing official reports containing increasingly insignificant and petty accusations against each other. I wrote a column on the reports that had them degenerating to point where the professors finally accused the president of farting in the presence of women, and the president responded by blamed the fart on the head of the faculty Senate. I knew what was next. I was called before the university's communications board for a reprimand. This was my next column.

You Mean I'm not in Good Taste?

"Recognizing the fact that (The Plainsman) has circulation off the campus, care should be taken to follow standards of good taste. Vulgar, coarse, and uncouth expressions have no place in it."

(from Policies Governing the Publication of the Plainsman, part 3 - section B)

I was asked to appear before the Auburn University Communications Board on Dec. 3 because my Nov. 18 column contained the word "f-rt." (Don't worry - there's no gag-rule on. I just don't want to spell the word out completely and be accused of sensationalism.) Anyway, the board wasn't too bent out of shape. They expressed their views and then listened to mine, and that was that. They only wanted to check on me and make sure I wasn't getting too crazy with power. That sort of thing.

I have no problem with this. The board members have a job to do, and they do it well. Part of this job is to reflect the norms and mores of the institution and culture they represent.

My problem is with the warped value system our culture has, especially when it comes to communication. Why is it that if you knife a woman in a movie, it's rated PG, but if you swear at her it's rated R, and if you make love to her it's rated X?

Why are violent words accepted in our society while words pertaining to bodily functions are not? We can't say "f---," but if we add some harmful force, it's perfectly acceptable to say "rape."

America has two types of people, word-thinkers and idea-thinkers, and the word-thinkers are in control of our values. To word-thinkers, it's better to spell out objectionable words instead of saying them. But here's an interesting question: is it OK to publish a quote of someone spelling out a word? Can we print, "You shouldn't say f-a-r-t"?

Word-thinking has become popular because it helps distract from the issue at hand. The idea here is that you can change the reality of something if you use nicer words. For instance: irregularity, femine protection, passed-away, bathroom tissue. The term "sleeping together" is used when nobody's getting a wink.

Word-thinkers like to use foreign languages a lot. If we want to make something sound great in America, we call it by its French name. This is because word-thinkers decided a long time ago that French is a classy language. No matter what you're selling, give it a French name and you double the price. Motor lodge: "chalet," steak: "filet mignon," side order of French fries: "vegetable a la carte," topless dancing: "follies bergeres," an undersized bottle of wine: "carafe." Want a gentle way to say "blow someone's brains out"? The French call it "coup de grace." Almost sounds romantic.

But just as we borrow classy words from the French, we need boogey-man language to dip into for our obscenities. Enter Anglo-Saxon. We have made obscenities of a handful of Anglo-Saxon words all dealing with nasty bodily functions and sex (sex being a nasty bodily function to those left out). The choice of Anglo-Saxon for our vulgarities and French for our top-shelf talk is based on as much reasoning as why we drive on the right side of the road. This is simply the way things are, and you better stay in your lane.

Though these people are extremely sensitive to sex and body-waste words, it's amazing how well they bear up under slangs for unkind behavior. This accounts for the tremendous comeback of the word "screw." This is probably because "screw" no longer represents intercourse, but instead means being overcharged by an auto mechanic.

Consequently, we can openly say, "My boss really screwed me yesterday," but we can't say, "My wife really s----ed me yesterday" (even if you only mean that she just bought five new dresses). This is because word-thinkers are offended by intimate acts but don't mind hearing about people hurting each other.

Our government is a perfect example of this. When we dropped napalm on Vietnamese villages, the radio logs were purged of any obscenities uttered by the pilots. The pentagon knew we wouldn't mind incinerated foreigners, but cursing while we did it would just be wrong.

In a culture limited to word-thinking, it is very important to learn the correct side of the road to drive.

Typing an article for the student newspaper, 1981.

Part Three

Cub Reporter

Montgomery, Alabama 1984-1986

Fresh out of college, I began writing obits and three-car crackups as a cub reporter. Meanwhile, I started work on my novelist muscles, composing short essays at home in my spare time. After I had enough jewels, I brought them to my editor and announced I wanted to become a humor columnist. He was so impressed he immediately said he couldn't pay me anything for them. Sounded fair. My column was called "From the Cheap Seats." ... Now here's the deal about newspaper columns: Given that you're writing for the entire populace, you need the broadest appeal and least controversy possible. Which took a lot of arrows out of my quiver. But it never stopped Mark Twain or Will Rogers or even Garrison Keillor. It would be an excellent exercise in controlled prose. So I slipped on some shit-kickers and developed my avuncular, Lake Wobegon voice. Of course I can't confirm or deny whether I went tongue-in-cheek on the genre to generate some clips, but here are a few of the results.

Cubans can't get to Havana by Red Level

They say you can choose your friends, but you can't choose your relatives.

You also can't choose the name of your town.

If you live in Lickskillet or Cluttsville, Alabama, then by God that's where you're from, like it or not.

The sillier the name of your town the more it seems people ask where you're from. If you live in a goofy town near a city, you broaden the dateline. "Where are you from?" someone from Atlanta asks his friend from Hueytown. "Er ... Birmingham."

Then there's Slapout. Because of this one place, no Alabamians are completely comfortable laughing as they drive through Yankee towns in Pennsylvania like Slippery Rock or Beaver Falls.

We've all wondered why some communities have certain names. Did the town planners get drunk one night? Did it appear in a religious vision to the minister that no one dared question?

One peculiar place is called Burnt Corn, either in memory of a crop failure or a bad cookout experience. The people of Bass, Chestnut, Pine Apple and Dill probably could pitch in.

Which brings us to the question of whether Alabama towns are really true to their names. Do they have a lot of trusses in Trussville? Do the people in Playball travel to Diamond a lot. If so. do they go by Canoe or Chrysler? Where do the nicest people live -- Pleasant Grove, Pleasant Hill or Pleasant Ridge? Do they fight about it?

Which is a safer place to live, Bear Creek or Pigeon Creek? And maybe Dry Forks should get together with Double Springs since they have an extra one. What about Red Level? It sounds it was inspired by a mine shaft or a missile silo: "Warning, now descending to ... Red Level."

Recognizing the importance of names, some local founders have copied famous foreign places, as if this will help. There is Athens, Waterloo, Bermuda, Cuba, Havana, Damascus, Demopolis, Madrid, Cairo, Troy, Rome and two named London ... all in Alabama.

Some places promote various community virtues, such as Equality, Independence, Industry, Excel, Brilliant, Enterprise, Reform, Unity, Providence and Liberty. (Universal town mottos: "The lady doth protest too much.") On the other hand, some townsfolk want to have a little fun in The Bottle, Scant City, Smut Eye, Nymph, Intercourse and Rash. Do I detect a progression there?

Still one town just wants to be Normal.

We also borrowed the names of a lot of American places. Unfortunately, they're the wrong places: Detroit, Burbank, Buffalo, Brooklyn, Cleveland, Memphis, Green Bay and Woodstock.

On the other hand, it might be nice living in a town that has the same name as you. In our state, a number of people are in luck: Bertha, Dan, Eddy, Edwin, Elrod, Florence, Gibson, Gordon, Grady, Hector, Herbert, Howard, Hugo, Jack, Kelly, Kent, Kimberly, Kirk, Leon, Leroy, Lester, Malcolm, Morris, Ralph, Randolph, Roxana, Theodore, Vincent, Waldo, Weaver, Glen Allen and Phil Campbell.

Other places make at least one person proud, but visitors might feel like they're trespassing: Pearces Mill, Millers Ferry, Stanleys Crossroads, Moores Bridge, Gantts Quarry, Whites Chapel and Hokes Bluff, which sounds like a good poker strategy.

In still other towns, the surveyors probably said, "What the heck -- let someone else name it," and nobody ever did. There's Section, Octagon, Half Acre, Seven Hills, Six Mile, Eight Mile and a pair of two-dimensional places called County Line. We have Central, Central City, Centre, Centreville, Centerpoint, Midland City and three places named Midway, none of which seem to be near the middle of anything. Northport is south of Southside, but Easton really is east of Weston. Two towns are tied with Five Points. There's Rainsville and Skyline which gave us Rainbow City, followed closely by Black, Indigo, Browns, Green Hill, Orange Beach, White City and Red Bank. Blue Springs and Yellow Pine formed Hazel Green.

After reading enough Alabama town names, they all start blending together. Oak Hill, Oak Grove, Grove Oak, Grove Hill, Hillwood, Woodville, Village Springs, Spring Hill, Spring Valley, Valley Head, Headland, Landersville, Springville, Brooksville, Mountain Brook, Millbrook, Milltown, Town Creek and Creek Stand.

And one last place to live in Alabama. Zip City.

Terrorists, wipe your feet

Welcome to *Southern Living* magazine.

In the world of *Southern Living*, there is no international strife or reports of bickering in the Reagan cabinet. Nobody visits Nazi cemeteries in its pages. Instead, we learn how to express our personalities through gourd carving. Life is syruply relaxed in *Southern Living*, the way we like it down here. Unhurried. Friendly. Quaint. In *Southern Living*, men are continually building water-repellant native-pine sun decks and marching in Civil War parades.

But in the fast-paced northern world of *Time* magazine, everything is urgent, stomach-churning madness, rude and phony people.

In the world of *Time* we are introduced to Carmine "the Snake" Persico, an alleged Mafia boss, and a gang of brutal Japanese heroin smugglers. We flee over the next few pages and find ourselves facing gasping crowds in India and Union Carbide officials with dopey stares.

The world of *Time* is not a healthy one.

Truck bombings in the Middle East, right-wing death squads in El Salvador, corrupt, drug-frenzied Mexican police implicated in the murder of an American agent. This is no way to relax before eatin' vittles.

Thank heavens Montgomery lives in the world of *Southern Living*. We move at our own pace, with our own people. No articles about break dancers or freaks with Cyndi Lauper rainbow hair in *Southern Living*.

And no Bo Derek.

Instead, we receive information about how to live like a family. "Mold a Chocolate Greeting Card," "Use a Rug to Direct Traffic" and "Enjoy the Zest of Citrus." Now these are articles.

Why should we bombard ourselves with the mainline hysteria of the Ayatollah and his Temple of Doom when we can "Microwave the Light Way"?

And since when did *Time* ever tell us how to make a casserole with macaroni and corn chips? Although *Time* now owns *Southern Living*, the magazine's covers are the first clue that something is still terribly different between their two worlds.

Who wants to see graphic images of overseas massacres and the etched faces of lying politicians when we can have six-color photographs of victory gardens and steaming crock pots? Besides, *Time* politics is all wrong for down here. While *Time* writers above the

Mason-Dixon inked out their wisdom on the fight against pestilence, Montgomery voters were passing measures to deal with the boll weevil menace.

People magazine is no better. In the world of *People*, defrocked Miss America Vanessa Williams tells readers, "I am not a lesbian and I am not a slut and somehow I am going to make people believe me." Frankly, Montgomerians couldn't care less what Miss Williams does in her personal life, as long as she tells us how to get more zest from our citrus.

But alas, she provides us with no such information. Instead she "lashes out at porn king Bob Guccione: 'I won't let that man destroy me.'"

Too bad. Lashing somebody to ribbons, even a porn king, is not what Montgomerians want to hear about in their spare time What we want to know is how to turn a dingy garage into a den, or vice versa.

Besides, the *People* world is silly. We learn of a summer camp for Cabbage Patch kids and see "Dynasty" star John Forsythe sucking on a tennis ball at some star tournament. A two-page advertisement promotes "beige" cigarettes. What does it all mean?

Montgomery is not an *Esquire* magazine city either.

Esquire doesn't seem so bad at first, with its advice on serving lamb and drinking gin, but then we are told of the effects of jockey shorts on fertility. And why do all the male fashion models pose with irrelevant objects such as dueling pistols and cricket bats?

Finally, Montgomery gives up on the *Esquire* world during an interview with LeRoy Neiman. The pop-sports artist is whining about a newspaper photo taken of him stuffing his craw with sushi.

Stop whining, LeRoy, and be a real *Southern Living* man. Discover the epiphany of biscuits.

Self-improvement: the new anti-war movement

Thank heaven we can be selfish again -- and feel good about it.

We've outgrown those childish 1960s concerns for the environment, our fellow man and the future of human rights. Now, as America's values mature, we understand where the energy of our ambitions should be focused -- on us. That's right. The president has made us feel good about ourselves again. If people in some underdeveloped nations are suffering, we'll just send them Helen Gurley Brown's "Having It All," an ode to career success, good looks, and romance on-the-go.

This shift in values hit full speed as yuppie-oriented television commercials for luxury cars began featuring Motown songs about suffering in the ghetto. So that's what the Four Tops really meant.

Faced with this tidal wave of disgusting narcissism, I quickly snapped into action. I joined in. Whenever I detect a hideous national trend -- and am in danger of being left out -- I retreat to the mall bookstore, the nerve center of breaking American culture. My trip revealed the end of the neighborly concern "I'm O.K., You're O.K." books. They've been replaced by "Looking Good," "Dressing Rich" and "How to Pick Up TWO Girls."

Being a new member of the self-improvement set, I dove into the nuclear proliferation of guide books: How to diet, how to lose weight by eating everything and drinking 12 glasses of water, how to meet the right people, how to avoid the wrong people, how to select a wardrobe and keep it lint-free, how to make good cocktails, how to kick alcoholism, how to grow a victory garden on your terrace, how to destroy rivals and keep smiling, how to make money off the stupid, how to make your husband lose weight without him knowing about it, how to find a spouse in a roomful of losers, how to make low-blood sugar work for you, how to avoid dropping dead, and how Roger Staubach turned his garage into a gymnasium.

The key for self-improvement authors is to tell readers exactly what they want to hear about their personal possibilities, no matter how hopeless the odds. The following titles are available on local shelves.

For those who need a complete overhaul: "Personhood -- the Art of Being Fully Human," "New Guide to Rational Living" and "Your Skin and How to Live In It." For those already chic, designer regimes: "The Scarsdale Medical Diet," "The Pritkin Program" and "The Beverly Hills Diet" (something to do with pineapples), "Dr. Abravanel's Body Type Diet," and "Suzy Prudden's I Can Exercise Anywhere" and annoy everyone.

Others want more than a health plan -- they want a miracles breakthrough: "The Revolutionary 7 Unit Low Fat Diet" ("Enjoy potatoes — even a drink"), "Dr. Atkins Diet Revolution," (sequel to "Dr. Atkins Nutrition Breakthrough"), "How to Lower Your Fat Thermostat," "An Alternative Approach to Allergies," "Do It Yourself

Shiatsu" (the ancient art of poking yourself, with a new introduction), and "Super-nutrition," now obsolete with the publication of "Mega-nutrition."

For the hopefully gullible: "Think Yourself Thin," "The Four Day Wonder Diet" (lose 10 pounds in 96 hours with grapefruit and hard-boiled eggs), "Lose 10 Years in 10 Days," "Better Health with Self-Hypnosis," "Diets Don't Work" and its yin-yang publication "The Only Diet There Is" (by Sondra Ray, author of "I Deserve Love.") The back-stabber on the way up has "Goodbye to Guilt," "Creating Wealth," "Getting Yours," "A Part-time Career for a Full-time You," "See You at the Top," "How to Write a Million Dollar Memo" ("Communicate Effectively! Get Everything You Want") and, "Confessions of an Advertising Man."

Shopping for the hypochondriac who has everything? "Mind Over Backache," "How to Stay Out of the Hospital," "Let's Get Well," "The Prevention of Incurable Disease," and "The Save Your Life Diet."

For the free-spending lush: "The Joy of Being Sober" and "Games Alcoholics Play" (checkers?), and the fool and his money: "How to Start a Conversation and Make Friends" (that'll be $19.95 friend).

We now have social-climbing sacraments: "Marrying Up" -- a checkbook guide to the altar, which wouldn't be complete without "Enticements: How to Look Fabulous in Lingerie." Which means you'll need "Check List for a Perfect Wedding," addressing such topics as "How do I cope with the receiving line if my parents are divorced" and "Planning a wedding in a meadow." If you made mistakes the first time around, there's always "The New Etiquette Guide to Getting Married Again."

And finally, for existentialists or fans of atrocious syntax everywhere: "Live Longer Now."

Old friends remember when we couldn't play the violin

We promised we would never forget our old friends. But the reality of our computerized, mobilized society is that we must draw the line somewhere. Not only do we forget old friends, we must consciously discard them like our favorite pair of worn-out socks or Grand Funk Railroad albums.

This is the sad truth of life in the 1980s, where our jobs shuttle us between cities and we meet a new cast of "friends" every six months. But the arrangement does have its advantages. For one, new friends know us only as we are now, not as the idiots we were -- just as our upcoming friends in the next decade won't know all the bonehead stunts we're pulling now.

As a rule of thumb, a sizable turnover in friends is the key to maintaining respect.

It has been said that life is like walking onto a stage, being handed a violin and told to perform. At first we have no idea how to play the instrument and everyone yells, "He stinks!" and throws rotten fruit.

But after a few years of practice we become excellent violinists. We've got a large crowd applauding our every note. Then a few "old friends" walk in and say, "So what? I remember when he stunk."

It's much harder to impress our first audiences. I remember this friend in kindergarten who sat in the back of the room and ate library paste. He's now a bank executive or something fantastic, but no matter how expensive his suits, I still see him with that goofy grin and milk-white smudges on his cheeks. Needless to say, I was one of the old friends he mysteriously lost contact with. I knew too much.

But although we lose touch, we never really lose friends. Relationships we haven't tended to in years are simply on inactive status.

A handful of times each year, these old friendships are reactivated, usually by unexpected, long-distance phone calls from people we used to know as "Wheels," "Skip," "Boopsy" or "The Mooner."

Sometimes they call to tell us they'll be passing through town. We invite them over for dinner.

Dinners with old friends are special. Spare no expense. Replace the soap in the bathroom. Shove stuff under the bed. The old friends are coming.

We love these events because we get to find out what has happened in our friends' lives. Most of these dinner guests fit into the following categories:

- The friend who used to tell you how to run your life and tries to sell you insurance after dessert.
- The friend who used to be the star athlete and is now in worse shape than you are.
- The friends whose divorce you correctly predicted after the last time they came to dinner.

- The friend who brings a different woman to each dinner and winks at you as he's leaving.

- The friend you were glad to know because he was richer than you — and you now hate because he's incredibly richer than you.

- The friends who talk about their costly overseas vacations and then ask where you went last year.

- The friend who spends way too much time in the bathroom and tells you why.

- The friend who tells you the girl you used to go steady with in school is now sleeping with everyone.

- The friend who is evasive about his occupation, makes several mysterious phone calls, leaves before dinner and is never heard from again.

Dinners with old friends start with drinks. Drinks help old friends tell funny old stories.

Three years ago I was at my old friend Bill's house for dinner. Several of his new friends were there, too. They told funny stories about Bill, but I had a funnier one. I told them about Bill sitting in the back of the classroom eating library paste. I laughed and Bill's new friends laughed and we drank some more and Bill spilled the gravy boat in my lap.

In 1984, I drove to Georgia to freelance an article on the national spectacle of the summer.

Lost, Stupid Out in Full Force

ATLANTA -- The Michael Jackson experience rolled into town last weekend on a $100-million wave of zillion-selling hit records, werewolf videos, burlap sacks of Grammy Awards, singed hair, hyperbaric chambers and rumors of bizarre pigmentation experiments.

The Victory Tour, featuring the numberless "Jacksons," is only in its eighth week but has shattered all records by playing to an estimated combined audience of more than a million. Equally staggering is the $28 price tag for even the worst seats.

Most tours are described by how many cities the groups cover. Not Michael. He plays states and sometimes entire regions. Official Jackson policy is not to announce any concert within a two-state radius of another show until the first one has played. This piece of Jackson trivia was revealed outside Fulton County Stadium by a man who identified himself as the photographer for Jermaine Jackson's attorney. The "in" thing on the tour was to have an impressive connection of one sort or another, and the photographer, being merely two seismic leaps removed from a genuine Jackson, was in high demand among the women with loose morals and no tickets.

The more obscure the connection, the more important the person acted. Credentials flapped from their lapels and belts and lanyards: hundreds of personal guests, producers, security guards, lawyers, accountants, technicians, hired flunkeys, private gurus and assorted hangers-on. One man in a turban told me was the only one allowed to cook Michael's food, and it was flown in from some place without electricity.

This cast of boobs in tow were only rivaled by the little people outside, mashed up against entrance gates, hysterically waving arms through the bars like they were escaping the Khmer Rouge. Some well-meaners passed out literature that said the real "Thriller" was Jesus.

"These same people were at the Knoxville concert," said the photographer. "They were carrying large signs that said Michael Jackson was a Satanist. They're weird people." He shook his head and changed the subject to his attorney friend. "They're having a private party upstairs after the concert," he said, gesturing toward the rafters in a manner that set forth the class distinction between us.

Next to him stood a man clad in leather pants, a leather jacket, leather boots, with a single gold earring. From his shoulders hung an array of four expensive cameras, all with telephoto lenses. No accessory bag and not a single pocket in his ultra-tight clown suit for filters or film. He was connected. For the entire concert he milled with the turban-cook and other various factotums, never taking a picture.

The only thing worse than connected people were those who weren't but wanted to be.

"We're with the television station," said two girls trying to persuade the press coordinator to let them in. "We're supposed to be over there helping." They finally wilted under the gate-keeper's gaze and were dismissed with a flick of the wrist.

Then there were the imitators. The audience was a blizzard of cheap Michael wanna-bes, all doing their best to find themselves by being someone else. Moonwalkers slinked backward in the stadium aisles, past legions of eight-year-old white boys with blond hair wearing spangled commodore jackets and sequined gloves purchased by parents with too much money and too little sense. No doubt about it, the lost and the stupid were out in full force for this one.

It emblemized our times, a desperate search for the self-definition that we had lost somewhere between the Apollo landings and the pet rock. They had been wandering without identity for years, through the entire '70s, shrugging off politics, fleeing serious religion and questioning why they should even continue to live.

Then a few years into the new decade, they rediscovered something that Gave Meaning to All.

The Jackson 5.

Later in that same Orwellian numbered year, I drove to New Orleans for another freelance piece.

It's a Small World After All

NEW ORLEANS -- An unidentified man forces open the door of a gondola at the 1984 World's Fair, waving a gun hundreds of feet above the Mississippi River.

"That had some people concerned," said a fair spokeswoman. Actually, the man was performing a stunt for television, but not all the spectators below realized it was staged.

This is one of several mistaken impressions that special World's Fair phone operators must straighten out. One chronic clarification is that the fair isn't a "fair" at all.

"Technically, it's the Louisiana World Exposition," says Kathline Branning, a public relations official for the event, "but it's easier to call it the World's Fair."

Branning said there is some kind of difference between the two categories, although she doesn't know what it is. She said the official distinctions between a fair and exposition have been established by the Bureau of International Expositions in Europe, but apparently they aren't sharing.

Another false rumor circulating in tourist circles is that the fair would be shut down, belly-up from financial bunglings.

"Have we heard the rumors?" said Branning. "Yes, we have -- and we've been battling them since the fair opened."

She maintained that the fair would indeed stay open, as scheduled, until Nov. 11, adding that those who miss it won't have another chance to see one in this country until the 1992 Chicago Exposition.

But for those who do make the trip to the Big Easy, a gentle heads-up. For the past six months, the city has been in the grips of a running battle -- or strained marriage – between the fair and the French Quarter.

On certain weekends this summer, the fair was a tomb -- its patrons lured away by the revelry of the Quarter, with its promise of untold human titillations to those who will only stay up a little longer and throw away a few more dollars. At other times, however, Middle America glutted the fair with thousands of Middle Americans, leaving the exotic dancers on Bourbon Street to sit in empty bars, drinking the house liquor and talking politics.

There is no gauge to determine which attraction will draw a crowd on any particular eve. Otherwise predictable people who enter the Crescent City find themselves under some unexplained Delta voodoo that leaves safe behavior out of the question. It's something in the Mississippi air or the beignets or maybe the ghosts of jazz funerals. And even the fair's executives are not immune.

Two Saturdays ago, the top headline on the New Orleans Times-Picayune read, "Ex-fair exec indicted in kickback scheme." Authorities claimed that a former marketing official of the expo had bilked the project by fraudulently licensing the fair logo and pocketing some of the money. The day after that news broke, the fair was mobbed by 66,971 people, the largest attendance in three months. Coincidence? I posed the question.

"I don't know what to credit that attendance with," said Branning. She noted that the only three days with higher attendance were the grand opening, July 4th and Japanese Fireworks Day, whatever that is.

Although the fair was jammed that Saturday, the Quarter siphoned most of the business the night before. In one Bourbon Street establishment a stripper was soliciting dollar bills for her G-string, claiming she was an official licensed product of the World's Fair. She, however, was not indicted.

"We've had a few more customers because of the fair," said the entertainer. "I think it's been good."

However, the whiskered night manager of an economy hotel on St. Charles Street disagreed. "You've got the same number of people coming to New Orleans and their money is being split between the fair and the Quarter. They're slitting each other's throats and it's no good for anybody." Then he looked in the direction of the river. "The fair's six blocks up the street, but the first two blocks are rough. Don't stop and talk to anybody. And if you bring any girls back, give us their first names and register them as your wives."

The curious were 30 deep at the fair ticket line outside the entrance gate flanked by two giant, topless mermaids -- the objects of continuing controversy. A short, stubby man was eager to talk as he waited in line. "Actually I've participated in the fair. I'm a cook, Cajun food," he said. "They don't have real Cajun food here, but it's not that bad."

He pulled out an American Express Gold Card to pay for his tickets as he explained why the fair has been good for the city. "The fall is a typically slow time for business. The fair has kept people coming into the Quarter."

And for those who grow weary of the Quarter's debauchery, the fair provides refuge if nothing else. The $15 cover charge serves to skim off the riff-raff and bottom-feeders that instinctively collect wherever drink and song flow freely.

Foreign correspondent gig, Central America 1986, when Reagan
sent the Alabama National Guard to Honduras as a shot across
the bow of the Sandinistas in Nicaragua.

Part Four

Magazine Columnist
Tampa, Florida, 2002-2005

After my fourth book came out, so did a new glossy magazine called Tampa Bay Illustrated. They asked me to write the monthly back-page column about local matters. Also, TBI was the kind of magazine with ads for ten-thousand-dollar kitchen counters and custom media rooms, hence the final column.

And the Votes Are In

Here we are, dear reader, second issue.

Can you believe it? It's all happened so fast. Who would have thought that our first issue would be so explosive and dominant as to create a sea change in the Gulf Coast advertising marketplace, leaving the newspapers and TV affiliates in disarray, their tearful staff members wandering silent offices aimlessly in confusion and fear?

Rumor has it that they will all soon cease operation, and repo men are now lining up to cart off desks and unscrew track lighting. Of course I started the rumor, but that's just me, always positive.

Which means we must pick up the pace over here at TBI to fill the yawning void. Magazines usually wait a year before their first annual Best of Tampa Bay issue, but not us.

You've seen all the plaques next to the cash registers at local shops and restaurants, just over the toothpicks and bowls of chalky mints. And exquisite particle-board treasures they are, engraved with accolades saying that whatever it is these people do, they do it better than anyone else in two counties. These are indeed coveted honors, and the benchmark criteria for businesses to win such awards are lofty and rigid: They must buy an ad.

Then the magazine makes a list of advertisers and creates a category for each.

Best Cuban Restaurant Operated by a Non-Cuban.

Best Non-Cuban Restaurant Operated by a Cuban.

Best Pet Grooming Service Whose Owner's Last Name is a Palindrome.

But you won't see that in this upstanding magazine. No, you won't see categories like:

Best Novel By a Columnist for Tampa Bay Illustrated: Triggerfish Twist, available in fine book stores everywhere, the perfect gift for all occasions.

Because we have standards.

We also do things differently. You probably remember from the last issue all those pre-paid "bind-in" cards asking you to vote for "Simply the Best." What a response! We took the mountains of completed cards to a germ-free clean room, where they were meticulously collated, tabulated, indexed, sealed in notarized boxes and escorted under armed guard to my office. But I was behind deadline so I threw them in a dumpster. Then I undertook a deliberative process of staring at a blank computer screen while fiddling with a swinging set of novelty clacking balls on my desk, and the results are finally in! Here we go, dear reader, the roll call of our inaugural "Simply the Best" winners:

Best Place to Meet Singles: along the Bayshore balustrade.

Best Place Not to Meet Singles: Orient Road Jail.

Best Damning With Faint Praise Chamber of Commerce slogan: "Tampa: America's Next Great City."

Second Best: "Tampa: Gateway to Lutz."

Best Baseball Team: Rays.

Best Hockey Team: Lightning.

Best Football Team: Visitors.

Best Peaceful Place to Commune with Nature: Egmont Key.

Best Global Theater Operations Center with Multiple-Warhead Thermonuclear Access and Command: MacDill Air Force Base.

Best Facial-Recognition Software: Ybor City.

Best Miracle: U.S. 19 plate glass Madonna.

Second Best Miracle: Glazers hire coach.

Best Public Sign Nobody Understands: Bayshore, "Tampa, sister city of Baranquilla, Colombia."

Best Place to be in a Crowd: Gasparilla Parade.

Best Place to be Alone: Rhonda Storms' mind.

Best Demolition of Perfectly Good Structure: (tie) old Tampa Stadium, Harbour Island People Mover.

Best Surreal Experience: Melting clocks ("The Persistence of Memory") Salvador Dali Museum.

Second Best Surreal Experience: Melting Olympic bid ("The Persistence of Turanchik") Exhibit now closed.

Best Place to Find a Parking Spot: Junction of I-4 and I-275

Best Facility, Major Sporting Event (modern era): Raymond James Stadium, Super Bowl XXXIII

Best Facility, Major Sport Event (classic era): Port Tampa, Spanish-American War

Best Place to View a Plane Sticking Out of a Downtown Building: Ballast Point Pier

Best Historic Landmark, European: Fort Brooke Parking Garage.

Best Historic Landmark, Native-American: Water tower with giant arrow, Seminole Bingo Palace

The particle boards are in the mail.

You Can't Get There from Here

I love driving.

I love driving because I live in Tampa Bay.

And if you live here, you better love driving or you better move. We're nominally all one big community, but the bay spreads out some of the trips like you're traveling between states in New England.

A few years back, St. Petersburg hosted the Final Four college basketball tournament. There was a lot of carping about driving distances between the area's attractions. A lot of these were New York types used to getting taxis, which you can't do here. Try taking a cab from Busch Gardens to a Greek restaurant in Tarpon Springs and it would be cheaper to buy a car and trade it in at the destination.

To me, all this driving means something else. Bridges. I love any excuse to cross the bay and drink in the breathtaking place where I live. Cargo ships sailing under the Skyway from the glistening Gulf, silver jets clearing the Courtney Campbell at sunset, the lighted red letters of "Misener Marine" reflecting in the midnight water across the Gandy.

I've even developed a routine to nurture these drives. My heart accelerates as I approach the Howard Frankland Bridge. I slip on polarized fishing sunglasses for needed enrichment of the magenta end of the spectrum, popping a *Miami Vice* soundtrack in the CD and bobbing my head to Jan Hammer, speeding up or slowing down to synchronize the song's peak with the bridge's apex. It's a carefully refined strategy designed to maximize aesthetic appreciation, distinguishing me from all the bozos around me on the bridge bobbing their head to their own stereos.

Driving around Tampa Bay is about a set of familiar names. Dale Mabry, LeeRoy Selmon, Fletcher, Klosterman, U.S. 19, the Tamiami Trail, Malfunction Junction (what's your function? Cracking up cars and semis and buses). It's about bumper stickers: "My child beat up your honor student," "Rehab is for quitters."

Driving around Tampa Bay is a good way to get to know the personality of the community: the police chases, parking lot fights, crashes, hand gestures that escalate like the assassination of Archduke Ferdinand. It's like being in a permanent studio audience for *COPS*.

Driving around Tampa Bay is about checking out the other drivers and guessing which ones haven't had sex the longest. Is it the guy in beat-up Datsun with gold wire hubs that cost more that the car? Or the '84 Camaro with purple neon tubes under the chassis?

Driving around Tampa Bay is about great stories. My favorite came from my nights as an editor at *The Tampa Tribune*. A reporter returned to the newsroom and told me about a driver who had gotten pulled over for speeding on the affectionately dubbed Howard Frankenstein. The police officer watched in amazement as the irate motorist ripped a new $400 laser radar detector off his dashboard and hurled it into the bay. The cop pointed at the sky. "We got you with the plane."

I'm in my car right now. It's an extremely dull car, marketed with TV ads using up-tempo rock music and quick-cut photography so you can't get a very good look at the vehicle. I'm heading down to Eckerd College, writing this article on a clipboard in my lap. Which is another reason I don't mind driving. I make productive use of the time, jotting down ideas, edit a story or two, maybe write a column for this magazine. Which is also how I miss exits, and now I'm heading over the Skyway to Manatee County. But what a view. Who could live anywhere else?

The vistas from way up here are incredible and I get out my digital camera to snap a few photos, another of my favorite drive-time activities. It's all coming together. Everything I love about this place. I'm having "a moment." I take some more pictures, and now just a few last scribbles on this clipboard while I cell-phone my editor that this column is almost done and–

Whoa! That jerk almost hit me!

But that's the price you pay to live here. They don't know how to drive.

How Time Flies

What a special day! Our big anniversary. And we owe it all to you, dear reader.

Can you believe it's already been 75 years since we put out that inaugural issue?

Yes, seven and a half decades, which makes this our sesquicentennial. Or maybe it doesn't; I can't keep that stuff straight. But that's not important. What matters is the ground we broke in 1928 becoming Tampa Bay's premier lifestyle magazine. And what perfect timing for that first issue, coinciding with Chaing Kai-Shek's sacking of

Canton, which we jumped all over in our cover piece, "Entertain with Cantonese flair!"

Much has changed since then. And much has stayed the same. We had a very different look, hand-cranking hot-type copies in the basement of a converted speakeasy across from the Kress building in downtown Tampa. The slick layouts would come later, as would most of the advertising, but not trademark articles like "The Right Wine for the Depression."

And who could forget December Seventh, 1941? That's right, the day we went glossy.

Bang! Bang! Bang! Tampa Bay Illustrated goes to war! The Social Scene pages became dominated by USO photos, and the magazine made its own sacrifice for the war effort using inferior glue in the binding process, which caused all the pages to fall out, but you, the valued reader, stood by us.

Victory in Europe! Victory in Japan! The troops come home; housing starts rocket. We bulge with ads for new developments. Of course back then it was Levittown instead of the portico Mediterranean manses of Puerto Vista Lago Bueno Boca Isles, but we were on our way.

Or so we thought. No one could have predicted the storm clouds that awaited. First, our float in the 1952 Gasparilla parade caught fire and ran over those tuba players, but the alcohol rumors could never be proven. Then, the following year, we were hauled in before the House Un-American Activities Committee after our feature, "Stubborn Rust Stains: The Real Red Menace."

It only made us stronger. We moved out of that dank basement and into new digs across the Bay. It was a golden era. Sock hops. Elvis. TV was still just black and white, but that didn't stop our "Ideal Media Room."

Into the 1960s: "Groovy Closet Concepts," "Trippin' on Custom Hardwood Staircases." The future never looked brighter. The Age of Aquarius. Man landing on the Moon. "Space-Age Dream Kitchens."

The Seventies and Eighties flew by. We just got bigger. The Nineties dawned, the world changed forever, and TBI was there. "Life after the Soviet Collapse: Avoiding the Top Five Accessorizing Mistakes."

Which brings us to the current moment. Just look at the quality in these pages, particularly the last one. This is no accident. Seventy-five years of sweat and perseverence went into the shimmering product you now hold in your hands. So I'm sure you can understand if we swell a bit with pride at this (sesquicentennial?) milestone. It has indeed been an impressive run, and I don't mind mentioning it since no one else will. We've never followed the crowd, never sought the approval of the media elite and filled our office shelves with gilded trophies, because we don't play that kind of cheap politics. The other outfits hoard Pulitzers for dumb-luck pictures from Saigon and Kent State, but nobody photographs almond-crusted shrimp scampi the way we do.

Sunshine Skyway bridge, Tampa Bay, 2012

Part Five

Captain Florida

In 2003, Sarasota Magazine asked me to write a series of travel-guide pieces about the state. Here are a few.

Wet your Whistle

I'm often asked, "What are the best bars in Florida?" To be more precise, I'm never asked.

Bars hold a special place in our hearts and minds. Probably because they're places of mystery and intrigue. Bars are usually dark, somewhat exotic and, thanks to the miracle of modern alcohol, crammed with possibilities.

Sarasota Magazine first approached me in 1979 with the concept of selecting the best bars in the state, and I've spent the last twenty-five years on assignment. They had originally given me four weeks, but I told them I didn't want to do a shoddy job. Then we lost all contact, and I'm sticking with the CIA story. But I'm finally back and I have much to report!

With a drum roll please, my top ten favorite Florida watering holes:

1. No Name Pub

This 1930s joint is a Florida classic with all the elements. Used to be a trading post and brothel, and the bar itself looks like it was salvaged from a sunken ship. Part of the draw is that it's so remote and hard to find, which eliminates the yo-yos that stumble into great bars on more traveled highways and ruin them. It's way down in the Keys, tucked along a back road on Big Pine – an over-grown shack almost completely hidden by the foliage. Take Watson Boulevard and look hard on the left just before the Bogie Channel Bridge over to No Name Key. There's a little hand-painted sign and a screen door. This is the land of the endangered miniature key deer, and over the bar is the mounted head of a regular deer and a plaque claiming it's the largest miniature deer ever shot. Scribbled-on dollar bills and business cards cover the walls. The staff claims their pizza is the best in the universe, and it just might be. Finally, the No Name defines the perfect level of seediness every good bar needs: that level of human excitement that doesn't slide off the scale into personal danger and head lice. You'll find bikers in leather next to grandparents in sweaters.

2. The Hub

This downtown Tampa bar does slide off the seediness scale on certain nights, but it's one of the few places where that's actually a plus.

The clientele runs the whole spectrum, from day-laborers counting out change for a beer to lawyers and college students. The appeal is it's frozen in 1949, when it first opened, and remains one-hundred percent authentic noir. This is a living exhibit to everything Mickey Spillane stood for. It looks like a place you'd more likely find on a busy city corner in Chicago. Catch it before it's gone. But one warning: Words cannot describe how strong the drinks are. One is more than enough. Two and you're ready for surgery.

3. The Flora-Bama Lounge and Package Store

This ramshackle 1962 roadhouse straddles the Florida-Alabama state line on the Gulf of Mexico. Out front, there's a pay phone at each end of the building, in each state, to avoid long distance charges. It's a raucous place, home of the "interstate mullet toss" (throwing fish as far as you can for fun and prizes). Like the No Name, this place is way off the beaten path, and the people who make it here are not in a hurry to get anywhere else. An old peach windsock flaps over the roof to aid customers who arrive by parachute and seaplane. The Flora-Bama looks like it's falling down and going up at the same time. Old and rickety, but with newer additions built on over the years hodgepodge, like it was hammered together by enemies of the owner. (Personal note: I placed a couple of scenes from my novel *Hammerhead Ranch Motel* in the Flora-Bama, and the owners asked me to come and do a reading. Remember that scene in the *Blues Brothers* when the band performs in that country bar?)

4. Pete's.

Another oldie, this one from 1933 in Jacksonville. A block from the Atlantic Ocean, Pete's is one of those great beach bars that's ultra-dark inside with doors propped open to bright shafts of sunlight, reminding you that it's only 11 a.m. and, yes, you're a barfly. The celebrity photos on the walls tell you you're still in Florida, but a world away from Miami: Bobby Bowden, Vince Dooley, Steve Spurrier, Herschel Walker, Bo Jackson. Bear Bryant and Pat Dye walking through the woods with shotguns on their shoulders. Pete's also has literary connections. Hemingway drank here. John Grisham visited while working on *The Brethren* and even put Pete's in the book. To commemorate this fact, the bar has placed a sign over the table where Grisham sat. The name of the book is misspelled. That alone makes Pete's one of my favorites.

5. The Bull

This was a tough call. Many purists give the Green Parrot, a block over on Whitehead Street, the nod as Key West's best bar. And with valid reason. The Bull is located on Duval, Key West's version of Bourbon Street, which means its spacious, open-air windows overlook the throngs from Middle America dragging themselves up and down the sidewalk, wearing straw hats, carrying tropical drinks and otherwise conducting this daily traveling gong show of amateur-hour drinking that always ends with the horror of a bald accountant from Cincinnati climbing on stage with a reggae band to sing "I Shot the Sheriff." That's a mighty steep down side to overcome, but I believe The Bull is up to the challenge. Go during the week, the summer, off-hours, a hurricane – whenever the streets are empty, and you will see the magic. The vaulted first floor of this historic masonry building features a mural wrapped around the room that chronicles the island's history, and the counter is one of those battle-scarred wooden horseshoes. Plus there's nude sunbathing on the roof. If you leave for the restroom, the bartender sticks a note on your drink for nobody to touch it because you've gone to pee.

6. The Desert Inn

People just like to say Yeehaw Junction.

Go ahead and try it. *Yeehaw Junction!* See what I mean? It's the funny name on the map at the crossroads of U.S. 60 and the Florida Turnpike about fifty miles southeast of Orlando's theme parks. Not much there except a couple of gas stations, a discount travel reservation center in a *defunct* gas station, and the Desert Inn. The motel and restaurant (on the National Register of Historic Places) has been around for more than a century since Yeehaw was a different kind of crossroads. Cattlemen driving their herds stopped here, as did Native-Americans, railroad people and other assorted rugged individualists. So don't expect a tiki hut from Daytona. This is the Old Florida of the crackers, out in the proverbial middle of nowhere, dust and heat, where whiskey is preferred to a blue drink that comes out of a slushy machine. There's an entry on the menu called the Florida Combo: "turtle, gator and frog (deep fried) $11.95." Enough said.

7. The Delano

If there could be an opposite of the Desert Inn, it would be the Delano. This landmark art deco hotel underwent an inspired post-modern renovation several years ago, and the local contingent of nightclub-hopping shock troops responded with approval. Go at midnight on a weekend for the full effect, which is like partying in a Calvin Klein ad while on sacred Indian mushrooms. Long, gossamer curtains flutter out the front entrance. Just inside the door, a bald woman sits at the concierge table in a uniform from the Star Trek collection; to the right, a ten-foot-tall Alice in Wonderland chair holds two young models sharing a brown cigarette. Ahead, a long, dark hallway where more white curtains section off the lobby into "rooms" containing bars, additional furniture of unnatural dimensions and clutches of people in the shadows. "Son of a Preacher Man" is piped in from somewhere, and another super-model-type dances slowly in red light atop an elongated table. Out the back door on the lawn, two people sit in chairs on opposite sides of a life-size chess set. Behind them, glimmering under a half moon, is a swimming pool that becomes shallower and shallower until it is only six inches deep and full of cocktail tables and chairs. A barefoot waiter splashes out into the water to deliver a tray of drinks. Ah, tradition.

8. Pier 66

Okay, I'm busted. I'm a Travis McGee fan. And as any devotee of the John D. MacDonald series can tell you, Travis liked to unwind at Pier 66, which isn't really a pier but a seventeen-story hotel in Fort Lauderdale with a revolving bar on top. The late MacDonald, the godfather of Florida crime fiction, was a longtime Sarasota resident, so I presume he decided that if his books were going to draw tourists and ruin a place, it would be far from his backyard. MacDonald had McGee living on a houseboat at the Bahia Mar Marina, an actual place that you can see from the revolving bar. You can also see the beaches, the downtown skyline and the hundred-foot yachts from Europe moored behind Mediterranean mansions on the Intracoastal Waterway. Late in the evening, the bar pounds with the international fast-lane pulse of South Florida. Last time I was there, I was seated near the musicians' bandstand, next to two big-shouldered men wearing black T-shirts and black sport coats, two black attache cases on the bar in front of them. Probably mob, I thought, maybe even South American bagmen. The briefcases? Had to be laundered cash or disassembled sniper rifles. And I'm sitting right next to them -- boy do I feel street-seasoned! Then the men opened their briefcases, took out a flute and a soprano sax, climbed onto the bandstand and began playing Kenny G.

9. Seafood Bar

The world-class Breakers defines Palm Beach opulence and history. Build by railroad magnate Henry Flagler in 1896 to accommodate wintering tycoons, the hotel has numerous lounges where a bar tab can quickly put you into Chapter Eleven. But my favorite is the little place with a low-key name in the very back of the resort. The Seafood Bar faces a row of large picture windows overlooking the Atlantic Ocean. But there's something besides the awesome decor and location that distinguishes this swank setup. There are many bars that have aquariums, but here the bar *is* an aquarium. Clown fish swim under you napkin and car keys as you perfect the art of nursing a drink.

10. The Fox

In the tradition of The Hub, this south Miami bar is a noir museum. Dark red light with red vinyl booths, it looks like the kind of place Joe Pesci and Ray Liotta might walk in. Beer won't do; you have to order something on the rocks. And smoke 'em if you got 'em. It was founded in a 1946 and sits at 6030 South Dixie Highway. I don't remember much else.

Honorable Mentions:

- Cabbage Key Inn - Located atop an Indian shell mound in Pine Island Sound (Fort Myers area), this century-old inn is only accessible by boat or aircraft, keeping it special.

- Trader Jon's - Lots of bars decorate with memorabilia. This Pensacola bar literally is a museum, bursting at the joists with naval aviation stuff.

- Skipper's Smokehouse - Smoked fish, funky decrepitude and some of the best live blues in the country. What more can you ask from this Tampa joint?

- Crescent Club - Lack of pretension and a 1950s attitude make this place the perfect antidote for franchised fern bars.

- Everglades Room - Located in the historic Clewiston Inn on the underside of Lake Okeechobee, the bar features a faded Audubon-like mural of glades wildlife and takes you back to the politically incorrect days when Big Sugar was king.

No Vacancy

It is the path less traveled.

Florida abounds with historic markers, verdigris plaques and entire roadside attractions surrounding something momentous that used to be there, and even some things that weren't (I'm looking in your direction, Fountain of Youth).

All you have to do is follow the signs. What fun is that?

The true joy is researching history and sniffing down some unmarked location where someone or something famous used to be. The less people know about it, and the fewer indications of its renown, the more rewarding the find. That's the whole key: Simply occupying the space and imagining. Sometimes I'll just stand and grin in a vacant lot, maybe take a soil sample where Jim Morrison's childhood home was bulldozed and read a poem. But don't get the idea it's something weird.

By far, my greatest yields have come from old hotels. People can't just walk around all the time. The north has countless "George Washington slept here" inscriptions. Florida more hip. There are no streamers around the room where Keith Richards wrote "Satisfaction" after the Rolling Stones performed at Clearwater's Jack Russell Stadium in 1965 (It's in the old Fort Harrison Hotel, now the Church of Scientology headquarters). Then there's the nearby suite and the Sheraton Sand Key, where Jim Bakker and Jessica Hahn had their infamous liaison in 1980 -- room 538 for those pushing the ick factor. To push it even further, there's the hideouts where serial killers Andrew Cunanan and Eileen Wuornos holed up (Normandy Plaza, Miami Beach; Fairview Motel, Port Orange).

I've stayed a couple of times at the downtown Jacksonville Hilton during book festivals, and next time I'm definitely requesting room 1010. Elvis had a habit of requesting the same room in certain cities, and this was his home away from home on the St. John's River (There's now a modest commemorative sign on the door: "Elvis Presley Suite," but you need a special elevator key to reach that level) According to one story on the web, housekeepers cut his bed sheets into little squares and sold them like religious artifacts.

I've wandered the Don Cesar, the pink grand dame on St. Pete Beach, a favorite of F. Scott Fitzgerald and Lou Gehrig, where Robert DeNiro was filmed during *Once Upon A Time in America*. I've explored the vintage 1891 Tampa Bay Hotel, now the University of Tampa, where the museum exhibits sepia photos of Teddy Roosevelt, Stephen Crane and Frederic Remington hanging out of the veranda before sailing to Cuba in 1898 for the Spanish-American War / Hearst newspaper subscription drive. I dodged security to loiter behind the historic 1926 Biltmore in Coral Gables, near the swimming pool where Esther Williams performed and Johnny Weissmuller broke a world record before becoming Tarzan.

But my biggest intrinsic haul was a lucky trifecta I hit in Miami. That's right: The Lucille Ball Room, The Goldfinger Room, and the Beatles Room.

The Beatles topped my scavenger list. Most people recall that when they first came to America, they played the *Ed Sullivan Show* in New York. But what's often overlooked is their encore Sullivan performance a week later that drew an even larger TV audience. Back then, Miami Beach was a popular remote broadcast site for big network programs like the *Today Show*. I knew the Beatles had made their second Sullivan appearance in the Napoleon banquet hall at Miami Beach's venerable Deauville Hotel, but I could never find out which rooms they stayed in. Time to redouble my efforts. I caught a lucky break on a Beatlephile web site; they stayed on the eleventh floor. This was confirmed by additional search engine hits, which indicated three rooms. John and his wife in one, Paul and Ringo in a second. George was upset he had to share the third with annoying New York DJ Murray the K. But no room numbers. I called the hotel and said I had it narrowed down to the eleventh floor, and could they tell me the specific rooms the Beatles had used, but they apparently mistook me for one of the many nuts running around Florida these days. The trail ran cold.

I decided to skip that SAT question and move on to Lucy. I had learned in a great out-of-print book, *The Life and Times of Miami Beach*, that Lucille Ball and Desi Arnaz had shot some "vacation" episodes of *I Love Lucy* in Florida, where Desi got his start with Xavier Cugat's band. Back to the Internet, where I scoured descriptions of every Lucy episode until I found what I was looking for (Episode 160, first aired Nov. 19, 1956). Next, patience. I surfed the web to find a copy of the show. A month later, one popped up on ebay (what a country!). I studied the tape. It opened with a black-and-white aerial shot of the fabulous Eden Roc Hotel. Then inside one of the rooms. I watched and watched but nothing remotely distinct. But patience pays. After a few more minutes, the smoking gun! Lucy picked up the phone and ordered some food up to "room 919." Bingo. On my next trip down there, somebody was already staying in the room, so I took a picture of the door. (Most excellent footnote: They actually shot the motel scenes on a sound stage, but took the time to accurately replicate the three-room alcove at the end of Eden Roc's ninth-floor hallway. For those of you with a life, never mind.) Next, Goldfinger. But my fortunes soured again. Already had that tape, which I carefully analyzed for clues. The room scenes had been shot at an English set, but the exterior footage was filmed on location at the Fontainebleau Hotel. There was a particular balcony scene where Jill Masterson helps Gert Frobe cheat at cards before she is painted to death. I did my best to use the movie's visual reference points from the pool to the balcony and triangulate, but significant decimals of the math is fuzzy. Within the margin of error, it's along a five-room block in the middle of the south wing facing the Atlantic between floors four and six.

Back to the Beatles. I was batting one for two now, and this was the rubber match. I found another tape on the web: a rare, behind-the-scenes documentary of the Beatles' first trip to America, complete with *Hard Day's Night*-style clowning around in Paul and Ringo's room at the Deauville. It got better. Shots off the balcony of Paul shouting down to screaming groupies. There were landmarks. I called the hotel back. How many rooms are on the east face? They said ten. *Hmmm, three rooms out of ten, thirty percent.* I booked a suite in the middle and phoned an equally eccentric research friend who once located David Letterman's pickup truck in California from a brief film clip on the *Tonight Show*. I needed that kind of expertise. "The Beatles room?" he said. "I'm there." We checked in with all my tapes and electronic equipment for on-site comparison. Work proceeded at a feverish pace. Wires and cables ran everywhere from the TV; video gear and more tapes were piled on top of the cabinet. The maid thought we were involved in the porn industry.

We carefully analyzed every relevant scene but still no progress. We decided to clear our heads with some side trips: into the bowels of the main Miami-Dade Library, where early 1960s cross-street directories helped up locate Jake LaMotta's Lounge from *Raging Bull* (now a Lum's restaurant a block north of Wolfie's deli on Collins Avenue) -- then down Washington Avenue to the site where Desi had started the rhumba craze in the 1930s (the ballroom of the Clay Hotel on the corner of Espanola Way, also former home of Al Capone's local casino, rooms 128-138). Despite these ancillary successes, we couldn't get the Fab Four out of our heads. What were we missing? Then it hit me. An image from the video popped up on a mental projector in my head.

We immediately raced back to the room and reviewed the documentary again, frame by frame, like the Zapruder film. My thumb hit freeze on the remote.

"Shazam!" I got up and tapped a spot on the TV screen, just behind where Paul was throwing Saltines off the balcony to some seagulls. "Right there! See? You can clearly count the number of balcony railings to the end of the floor. It's the third room from the north.

We ran out the door and down the hallway and began counting rooms, 1111, 1112 , 1114 (the Deauville omitted 1113 because of superstition -- a critical trap we avoided). We dashed back into our suite and called the front desk. "Uh, listen, we don't really like this room ... But I'll bet eleven-fourteen is terrific ... It's available? We'll be right down! ..."

So we carted all our junk down the hall and were soon sitting on the foots of the beds in one of the Beatles' rooms, watching a video of the Paul and Ringo goofing around in the same room forty years ago. We glanced around. Little had changed. We opened bottles of beer, clinked them together and thought, yeah, now this is cultured.

The Right (Innocent) Stuff

Time has that way of healing.

It's been five months since Columbia.

I have two daughters, Erin, 6, and Kelly, 4, and I take them to space shuttle launches. It's our special getaway, just me and the girls. Late bedtimes, mega-snacks, unlimited playing at the official NASA Visitor's Center, the motel room looking like a rock star went berserk with a truckload of space souvenirs -- and that's just me.

I've been fascinated with the space program since I was a small child growing up near West Palm Beach in the 1960s, where I sat for hours in front of the TV set in a foil-wrapped cardboard box/space capsule, drinking Tang back when it tasted bad, and watching the around-the-clock coverage they used to give early launches (including several hours of a stationary shot through the open doors of a Gemini capsule of two astronauts lying on their backs). Then, after the countdown reached zero, I'd run out in the front yard and look north for the rocket.

I was hoping my girls would pick up the obsessive interest, but I didn't want to be one of *those* parents. So I just gave them the exposure. Luckily, they took to it right away. I guess they wanted to be like me, but it might have been all the really expensive space toys I bought them, the moon buggies and Apollo action figures and the giant $55 Saturn rocket with real-voice countdown that rumbles and vibrates on launch. Plus those full-tilt, unlimited ice cream slumber parties we had at the cape. Any kid will crack under that kind of pressure.

Erin soon said she wanted to be an astronaut when she grew up. Kelly still wanted to be a Bucs cheerleader, but was showing promise with the action figures.

I couldn't have been prouder.

So we were planning on taking another one of our trips to the cape for a launch this spring.

Then the footage from the sky over Texas. People gathered around television sets in public places once more.

When I got home, my older daughter said she didn't want to be an astronaut anymore.

My younger asked: "How are they going to put the pieces back together so they can be alive again?"

There were no good answers.

So we watched Apollo 13 for the twentieth time, because I wanted them to see a happy ending.

I had business on the road shortly afterward that took me to the cape. Driving up U.S. 1 through Cocoa, the American flags were back out, the advertising replaced on marquees in front of the fast-food restaurants and muffler shops: "Remember Columbia in your prayers" and "God bless the crew of Columbia."

Who couldn't feel bad? But I wondered: We see disasters on the evening news every night where many more people are killed. These were just seven. So why the big punched-in-the-gut feeling?

I realized my own reason as the days passed, and I watched, over and over, as the networks televised archive footage of the Columbia crew in training. It was something in those smiling faces.

Tom Wolfe coined "The Right Stuff" for the Original Seven Mercury astronauts. But back then, the stuff that was needed was the best test pilots with the least fear (John Glenn went up in a rocket that had a 40 percent track record of exploding). It also meant most were hard-drinking, fast-driving, macho, hang-it-over-the-edge daredevils.

As I watched the tapes of Columbia in training, I realized how much had changed. This was a completely different kind of "right stuff." No less courageous. But steady and dependable. Idealism and principles.

If the country was reduced to a small town, they would be the top of the high school graduating class, the most virtuous star students and athletes. The ones the town was pinning its hopes on to go out and do the stuff of dreams.

Then they were all gone in a blink.

I keep thinking of a bunch of corny themes involving "innocence." My own innocence as a child watching the definitely not innocent early astronauts. The innocence of all those roadside remembrances to the lost shuttle crew. The innocence of my children asking questions about the space program – and that I seemed to regain as I watch it all through their eyes.

That's the thing about innocence. It *is* corny -- when you don't have it anymore.

So we've decided we're going to take another one of our shuttle launch vacations to the cape, even though there won't be a launch.

First, right after we wreck the motel room with NASA paraphernalia, we'll hit the new Saturn V exhibit, catch an IMAX movie and take the bus tour out to the launch pads, that humongous crawler that transports the shuttle, and the cavernous Vehicle Assembly Building. (I took a similar tour when I was a child and still remember the bus driver's voice of authority over the PA saying that clouds sometimes form inside the building, and four-and-a-half baseball fields can fit on the roof.) Then we'll break from the attractions described in the tourist pamphlets and strike out on our own custom A-tour of local institutions. That's the thing about the Cocoa Beach area: it's really a small company town that's still old Florida, practically frozen in the '60s when astronauts zipped along undeveloped beachfront in Corvette convertibles. History preserved everywhere.

We'll eat breakfast again at the Moon Hut, the historic diner that was a favorite of the astronauts and launch teams, with a ton of space memorabilia on the walls. We'll have lunch at the Durango steak house, because it used to be the Mousetrap, the legendary and notorious nightspot, with more period memorabilia. And we'll order dinner at Bernard's Surf, "since 1948," because of -- you guessed it --

autographed photos of astronauts having dinner there (great Apollo-Soyuz stuff).

Our traditional sunset location is the 800-foot-long Cocoa Beach Pier, a popular launch viewing site since the beginning. The pier is actually more like a small boom town on stilts jutting out into the water. There are numerous restaurants and shops and a tiki bar at the end. And, of course, plenty of memories on the walls to keep a space afficionado occupied. Then we'll stay up late trashing the motel room some more, fueled by sodas and pouches of freeze-dried "Astronaut Ice Cream" from the NASA gift shop.

Day Two: No chance of running out of places anytime soon. We'll head back up A1A, past a street sign, "I Dream of Jeannie Way," to Alma's Italian & Seafood Restaurant. Most of Alma's stuff was lost in a fire, but there's still a faded photograph of Apollo 12's Alan Bean walking on the lunar surface in 1969. It's inscribed: "I was the first man in history to eat spaghetti on the moon, but believe me it didn't equal yours." Nearby is the Econo Lodge, which used to be the Cape Colony Inn, owned by the Mercury astronauts. There's still a lounge in their honor and a commemorative sign in back behind the pool and Chinese restaurant.

I'll have to pull over at Ron Jon Surf Shop, which used to be the venerable surf joint on the pier when the astronauts took up the sport in their down time, before it moved into a building so big and garish that the kids won't let me pass without stopping (they know about the space toys inside). Then we'll cross over to the mainland and cruise up U.S. Highway 1 toward Titusville, to a small waterfront park on Indian River Avenue, with big, gleaming metal monuments to the "Original Seven" Mercury astronauts and the "Next Nine" of the Gemini program, where the kids will wiggle their fingers inside the palm prints cast in bronze.

Before heading home, we'll put in some more time at the official NASA visitor's center, where they'll run around the "Rocket Garden" and through the full-scale shuttle mock-up. We'll roam inside the dimly lit gallery of manned spaceflight, staring in wonderment at early capsules that seemed so futuristic in their time and now look like primitive barrels that went over Niagara Falls.

Finally, we will visit the silent, polished-granite astronaut memorial on the northern edge of the center, with names like Grissom and Chaffee and McAuliffe. The three of us standing there in innocence.

And we will remember Columbia.

Astronaut Memorial, Kennedy Space Center, 2010

Part Six

Gun For Hire

Over the years I've written a wide variety of freelance articles for an equally varied a group of publications. They defy category.

Best of the Bay
(Weekly Planet, 2004)

What follows is a personal Julie Andrews list of my favorite things about this area, the simple pleasures, mostly free, some with nominal costs -- the kind of "attractions" we'd otherwise overlook because they don't require an $89 ticket and two-mile tram ride from the parking lot. The list is in no particular order, but I've decided to rank them because that seems to cause trouble.

1. Tampa International Airport, top deck of short-term parking (level 7). Perfect place to view space shuttle launches, especially at night. I saw the John Glenn launch up there and was stunned by the hundreds of other residents who spontaneously showed up. Until the manned launches resume, you can find NASA schedules of satellite launches on the Internet. Also great for spotting the orbiting International Space Station. At other times, the parking deck is a great vantage to catch a sunset, watch planes take off or chill and just flush your head, observing the handful of other people loitering with no apparent business and thinking, "Man, they're messed up."

2. Friendship Trail Bridge. Another stress reducer. This magnificent 2.6-mile span of the old Gandy Bridge was slated for demolition until rescued by an unlikely alliance of health-crazed joggers and beer-pounding fishermen. More great views that showcase our geography's natural beauty. Lots of dolphins, pelicans and afternoon electrical storms that get the all-important cardio-vascular up as you race down the bridge's exposed hump.

3. Fourth of July "people's" fireworks display, Gandy causeway. Mark your calendars! It's the best pyrotechnics display in five counties -- and it's interactive! I tripped over it by accident two years ago while driving over to Pinellas looking for an officially sactioned show. I approached that part of the causeway on the west side of the bridge featuring Jet Skis, free-range dogs, rebel flags and T-back hotdog vendors. Each Independence Day, the beach-goers stay after dark to ignite a week's salary of fireworks bought from tents along Dale Mabry Highway. And as Dave Barry says, I'm not making this up: I've never seen a fire truck "on patrol" before, but one was going up and down the causeway as people twirled sparklers next to piles of ordnance and

knocked over Roman Candle launchers, sending flaming balls horizontally through traffic. The best visual analogy is that bridge scene in *Apocalypse Now*, where all kinds of flares and tracers whizzed randomly over the river. My wife and I drove back and forth three times as these little comets zoomed over the hood. Best Fourth of July show ever. Keep the windows up.

4. Derby Lane. This grand dame of Tampa Bay's old social scene has survived since the 1920s. It seems hard to imagine now, but the "Lane" used to arrange huge promotional appearances by the likes of Jim Thorpe and Babe Ruth. But we are no longer in the golden age of the parimutuels, and many other tracks across the state have become a bit too, well, dicey. And mind you, I'm *all about* dicey. That's what makes Derby so special: a rare combination of keeping the place up without altering the historic architectural lines, which is what attracted the makers of *Ocean's Eleven* for the Carl Reiner intro scene. Hopefully it will be around for many more decades, unlike my beloved Tampa Jai Alai Fronton, where my favorite seats are now a lug-wrench display in The Home Depot.

5. The Coliseum, 535 4th Ave N., St Petersburg. Most of the old pre-World War II era ballroom dancing facilities are long gone, but we're still lucky to have one of the best. The Coliseum continues to host some oldie music shows, or you can visit during the annual antiquarian book show in March. Like Derby Lane, it's another survivor whose exquisite architecture attracted Hollywood filmmakers, adding to our sophisticated culture. In this case, the scene in *Cocoon* where Don Ameche break dances.

Dang, I'm running out of time and space here, so I'll wrap it up with a lightning-round of "the best of the rest."

6. Union Station, 601 N Nebraska Ave., Tampa. Another great transportation hub to visit when you have no legitimate business. Winner of the "Comeback from Sketchiness Award." Take the Amtrak out of here while you still can.

7. La Teresita, 3246 W Columbus Drive, Tampa. Plentiful, inexpensive Cuban home-cooking in another historic setting. Forgo the dining room for the double-horseshoe lunch counter experience.

8. The Tampa Theatre, 711 N Franklin St., Tampa. One of the state's only classic balcony theaters still showing movies. Since 1926.

9. The Bayshore Balustrade. From the psychedelic fish to the giant slinky sculpture, the "world's longest continuous sidewalk" along

Tampa's most coveted address is worth the stroll just to see what floats up to the seawall from the Bay.

10. Bern's, 1208 S Howard Ave., Tampa. Not a simple pleasure and definitely not cheap, but Tampa's world-famous steak house must be included for its positive-weirdness score. Outside, a warehouse; inside, a baroque brothel with medieval suits of armor; upstairs, dessert with Rod Serling. It can't be explained.

11. Port Tampa Library, 4902 W Commerce St., Tampa. The remaining, Greek-columned landmark of what used to be a sister city before it was all connected by growth.

12. Hotel Ponce DeLeon, 95 Central Ave., St. Petersburg. Venerable institution raised from the grave. Have to love the old hand-operated elevator and below-street-level piano bar.

13. St. Pete Beach Holiday Inn, revolving rooftop bar, 5250 Gulf Blvd, St Pete Beach. The Don Cesar down the street may be more fashionable, but why drink if you can't revolve?

14. R.I.P. The Chatterbox, The Hub (original location).

Comic Threat

(Mother Jones magazine, 1994)

Michael Christopher Diana probably wouldn't be your first choice to date your daughter or sister.

He has tattoos and long, stringy hair, likes the band Nine Inch Nails, sports a pronounced anarchist attitude, and fits most people's definition of, well, creepy.

And Diana gets into trouble. Recently, he was arrested in Orlando when he tried to pay for a horse-and-carriage ride with a $1 bill doctored to look like a $20 bill. His attorney says Diana was unaware of the forgery and charges were dropped when Diana agreed to a pretrial probation program.

But Diana's claim to fame is that he likes to draw. And the brutal images that come forth when he puts pen to paper have made the authorities in Pinellas County, Fla., want to lock him up: They tested his blood to see if he was a serial killer; they jailed him without bail while he awaited sentencing; they fined him $3,000.

What sent up red flags in the civil liberties community, however, was an extraordinary part of his probation sentence. The judge ruled that Diana's thinking had to be rehabilitated. To this end, he ordered that all Diana's personal papers be subject to unannounced searches. Anything Diana draws or any private thoughts he might want to write down may be seized without a warrant at any moment.

After working shifts at his family's convenience store in Largo, Diana liked to sit alone in his bedroom at his father's house and draw. The sessions often lasted until 3 or 4 a.m., and what emerged were brutal images incorporating penises, breasts, excrement, blood, and intestines, not to mention appendages and body cavities that just don't exist in the real world.

About six years ago, Diana started putting his harsher work together in a comic book 'zine he called "Boiled Angel," which he distributed to about 300 subscribers across the United States and abroad.

Some drawings in "Boiled Angel" stood alone, and others were strung together in story lines:

- A child is sodomized by his adoptive father, who is killed by the family dog. The boy thinks he's finally free until the dog picks up where the dad left off.

- A man looks at a pretty woman. In the next frame -- a montage – the man has the look of a psychopath and is surrounded by slivers of abstract images, including a nipple being sliced off by a knife.

- A youngster goes to church looking for a priest and gets semen squirted in his face by a giant penis. The child grows up emotionally disturbed, taking drugs and shoving a crucifix up his rectum.

Three years ago, one of the comics found its way into the hands of a California law enforcement officer. Parts of it reminded him of the then-unsolved Gainesville student murders. The book was forwarded to Florida, where state authorities sought out Diana and asked him for a blood sample to see if he was the killer. After laboratory tests dismissed him as a suspect, his comic was passed to the Pinellas County Sheriff's Office, which charged Diana under a Florida obscenity law.

Last March, he went on trial in Pinellas County court. The Comic Book Legal Defense Fund paid for Diana's defense by Tampa attorney Luke Lirot. Six citizens minding their own business around sleepy, retirement-oriented St. Petersburg were summoned to a jury box to look at penises and mutilation. "They were visibly shaken, visibly disgusted," Lirot said.

It's difficult to blame them. Diana isn't the boy next door; his artistic tastes, when compared to the mainstream, are completely off the meter. Whether it's death and excrement, or simply shapes that make no sense, most of Diana's material leaves viewers wondering, "What's wrong with this kid?"

Diana says he wants to open people's eyes by shocking them. For citizens who aren't seeking to jolt themselves--who are simply showing up at the courthouse to fulfill a civic duty--it's just plain offensive.

American courts have decided that rights of free expression cover a broad range of filth, hate, and violence. The sole trip wire that slams the First Amendment shut is sexually arousing material. In other words, you can be as disgusting and violent as you want, as long as nobody gets turned on.

As Pinellas County Assistant State Attorney Stuart Baggish, who prosecuted the Diana case, explains, a teen-slasher movie available at a video store would not be ruled obscene, because "it portrays violence in a gross way, but it does not portray sex in a patently offensive way."

According to the 1973 U.S. Supreme Court ruling in Miller v. California, material must pass three legal tests to be judged obscene. First, it must appeal to the "average" prurient interest in sex. Second, it must portray sex in a patently offensive manner. And third, it must have no serious artistic, literary, political, or scientific value. If any of the three criteria don't apply, the material is not obscene.

In Diana's case, the first hurdle was especially tricky. The drawings might repulse jurors, but get them horny?

The prosecution was helped by the 1966 case Mishkin v. New York, which involved the distribution of sadomasochistic pornography. The case set a precedent that material appealing to a deviant sex market need not arouse average viewers. (A humorous attempt to use the Mishkin exception took place in 1988, when Alabama prosecutors tried to prove the obscenity of a bumper sticker that read: "How's my driving? Call 1-800-EAT-SHIT!" The state brought in medical textbooks describing coprophagia and coprolalia -- the sexual enjoyments of eating excrement and uttering obscenities -- and used as expert witness a local professor who taught a course on abnormal sexuality. The state lost.)

Prosecutor Baggish used a similar strategy against Michael Diana, bringing in Tampa psychologist Sidney Merin as a state witness. Merin said that people "of questionable personality strengths" could be aroused by the comic book.

In an antiseptic legal world, Diana probably would have won. His cartoons may be gory and repulsive, but it's hard to imagine them arousing anyone. But as in many obscenity cases, both sides often abandoned points of law in favor of long-distance detours through legally irrelevant emotional territory.

Defense attorney Lirot emphasized an often obscured and sometimes contradictory element in Diana's work -- his concern about "victimization." Prosecutor Baggish told the jurors that if Diana weren't stopped he might become a mass murderer. (After the trial Baggish pointed out in an interview that serial killer Ted Bundy had blamed pornography for his crimes: "People said, 'Oh, my God, why didn't somebody do something about it?' In this case somebody did something about it.") Letters poured into the court from religious and family values groups such as the American Family Association and the Concerned Women for America. "The pictures … serve as a reminder that there will always be individuals that pervert and twist the meaning of freedom," wrote the Concerned Women's area representative. "The production of obscenity and violence against women and children is not freedom, but one step away from destruction."

In his summary, Baggish told the jurors that Pinellas County didn't have to accept "what is acceptable in the bathhouses of San Francisco and … the crack alleys of New York."

The jury deliberated for 90 minutes.

Guilty.

Ironically, what may have tipped the scales against Diana was the very political content that should have saved him. The overall message of "Boiled Angel" is one big spit at authority. It's legitimate speech under the First Amendment, but not very popular in Pinellas County.

Most pronounced is the comic book's virulent anti-Christian message, aimed particularly at the Roman Catholic Church. There are assaults on the Church over pedophile priests, as well as a lot of crosses (one with cartoon poop on it). There's a drawing of two eggs frying on top of a Bible, with the caption: This is your brain on religion.

According to Robyn Blumner, executive director of the American Civil Liberties Union of Florida, that political message should have saved "Boiled Angel" from an obscenity conviction. "But in this case," she says, "the very political message was inflammatory and helped convict Michael Diana."

Judge Walter Fullerton ordered Diana held in jail until sentencing. What made it peculiar was that he ordered him held without bail -- the norm for murderers and cocaine kingpins. Diana was only convicted of misdemeanors.

"I felt incarceration in jail was part of the sentence, so why not begin?" says Fullerton. "He learned some good lessons."

At sentencing, Baggish asked the judge to incarcerate Diana for two years, despite a prison-space crisis in Florida that has resulted in the ultra-early release of violent criminals. Fullerton instead chose three years of supervised probation. Diana would have to pay fines, do community service, and avoid contact with minors. But there was still one more catch.

Fullerton ordered Diana to follow a state-supervised program to rehabilitate his thinking. Diana was required to undergo psychiatric evaluation and take an ethics-in-journalism class. Finally, Diana was to submit to unannounced, warrantless searches of his personal papers by the police and deputized probation officers from the Salvation Army. Any drawings, any letters to family, any feelings Diana might want to keep in a diary could be seized.

Although random searches during probation are generally imposed only in drug and weapons cases, Baggish says it was natural to extend such searches to help reform an obscenity offender.

"Treatment is the most important part of the sentence," he says. Unannounced searches are needed to force Diana "to refrain in a rehabilitative vein from this conduct. To cure the psychological maladjustment, [it's necessary] to catch him in his true state."

It's not difficult to see why Diana's art might prompt questions about his mental health. But when is it appropriate for the government to decide that someone's thinking needs to be rehabilitated?

"I don't know of any time when such monitoring has been used on an artist," says the ACLU's Blumner. "It reminds you of mind control. The fact that the state doesn't like Michael Diana's attitude and will send him to experts and conduct searches is like legalized lobotomy."

There have been about half-a-dozen comic book obscenity cases in the United States, but most involved store owners--and nobody was ever ordered to stop drawing, says Susan Alston of the Comic Book Legal Defense Fund in Northampton, Mass. "Diana is definitely the first artist who's been banned as part of his sentence."

"That's absolutely illegal," says Richard Wilson, a national officer of the First Amendment Lawyers Association. He explained that the judge's sentencing order of "no ... creation of obscenity (drawings, writings)" amounted to unconstitutional prior restraint.

It's a sticky matter debating whether something is art. As the late shock-comedian Lenny Bruce said of obscenity cases, the expression often is art and the lawyers are really debating whether it's good or bad art. The jury is put in the position of punishing untalented artists.

And whether or not Diana has any talent is certainly debatable. Baggish describes Diana's work as "a kick in the head. It lacks any serious--underline serious--artistic or literary value."

"The jury made the decision; I didn't," says Judge Fullerton. "But if you looked at it, you wouldn't question their verdict."

Diana has a different view: "They asked the jurors what their idea of art was, and one of them said needle-point."

Diana's case is now on appeal, and the conditions of his probation are suspended pending a ruling by the circuit court, possibly as early as February. In a virtually unheard-of ruling, the Pinellas County appeals judge rejected a routine request by the American Civil Liberties Union to file a friend-of-the-court legal brief in the case.

At least for now, the excitement has died down. Diana is left sitting in his father's convenience store, wondering whether he'll have to resume paying off his $3,000 fine, chipping away at his 1,248 hours of community service, and visiting a psychiatrist.

"They want me to get mental help so I'll change," says Diana, "and I don't see how I could, because there's nothing wrong with me."

Thus far, Diana hasn't changed. He and his fiance Suzy Smith (whose local cable show was canceled after she aired a video clip of punk rocker GG Allin defecating on stage) recently posed naked for an underground 'zine. In the accompanying interview, Diana says he wants "to stay alive and try to cause trouble through my art or whatever I do, and hopefully corrupt some other people and make people realize they have the right to do whatever it is they're doing." Diana has even started work on a new comic called "Superfly."

Not far from the courthouse, in another part of Pinellas County, are other disturbing paintings and drawings. Although more complex and artfully rendered than Diana's cartoons, they share a number of thematic similarities.

The paintings include penises and breasts and disfigured buttocks. A severed head. Blood coming out of an eye socket and from anuses. One painting, "The Profanation of the Host," even mixes group homosexual activity with religious images.

But this collection of work is neither hidden nor under attack. On the contrary, it is proudly publicized as one of St. Petersburg's cultural crown jewels: the Salvador Dali Museum.

In 2008, ESPN asked me to write about the Auburn-Alabama football rivalry for one of their publications.

A Religion by Another Name

Auburn University. The Tigers, the Plainsmen, War Eagles – what the heck were we?

It was an especially pertinent question for me as I was raised in south Florida, which, with all the transplants at the time, was like growing up in an identity-free zone. Then I got an ROTC scholarship and found myself in the fall of '79 at "The Loveliest Village on the Plains."

It was my first exposure to the Deep South. Culture shock. It was no more distilled and concentrated than in something I soon discovered called SEC football. Or by another name, sanctioned madness.

Rabid pep rallies, ubiquitous parties spilling into the streets till dawn, alumni naming children Jordan and Hare (after the stadium), RVs arriving to begin tailgating on *Tuesday*. Frat boys going to the games in suits and orange-and-blue ties; sorority sisters dressed for a prom. ... Me in my T-shirt and flip-flops. Then I entered the stadium that first game, into this surreal sea of religious hysteria, and again had to recalibrate my cultural horizon.

But the full gravity of this feverish mind-set didn't sink in until a few weeks later. I had joined the student newspaper that first semester, and I had a humor column. I thought it would be a hoot to cull my outsider's perspective on the fanaticism and poke a little fun at AU football.

Whoops.

You could say the reaction was not good -- as in that photo of Mussolini and his wife hanging upside-down like pinatas. My phone rang non-stop; I was warned to stay away from the newspaper office; I slept under my bed in case lead came through the window.

Looking back, that last measure was an over-reaction. The Auburn community prides itself on sophistication. Had I been attending, say, the University of Alabama, I would have had to transfer. With police protection.

Fast forward: Senior year. I was now editor of the student newspaper. I never missed a game. I dressed in orange and blue. My throat was hoarse every Sunday morning. I'd long since become one of the very people I'd kidded about my freshman year. So what had happened?

It was something particularly Auburn. And it wasn't just football. Something about this bucolic paradise in the middle of east Alabama farmland. You can't live there for four years and not fall in love with the place, the people, the landmark clock tower, the bitchin' landscaping. Football was simply the common bond of loyalty to the place that nurtured us through a coming of age. And it was all ours. Because back then there were three types of people who lived in the state: Those who went to Alabama and rooted for Alabama, those who went to Auburn and rooted for Auburn, and everyone else who went to neither school -- and rooted for Alabama. From Mobile to Montgomery to Huntsville: Roll Tide bumper stickers and elephant flags and photos on restaurant walls of an unmistakable profile in a hounds-tooth hat.

That just made it better. What we had wasn't diluted. And I'm not just making lemonade. You saw someone in an AU jersey, it was real. And we definitely weren't spoiled. Many years had passed since the reign of Ralph "Shug" Jordan." Many tough losing seasons. Some schools border on open revolt if they don't make the title game, let alone win their conference. Not us. Nothing taken for granted, a bone-deep appreciation for anything we got. My senior year, we hadn't beaten our Tuscaloosa rival in a decade, ever since the miraculous "Punt, Bama, Punt" game back in '72, which we were *still* celebrating.

So by 1982, yes, I had come full circle. The Iron Bowl season finale against Alabama approached, and I wrote such a passionate editorial to support the team that it was criticized by a journalism professor at another school as "an invitation to riot." He obviously didn't know Auburn people. We don't riot; we just throw a lot of toilet paper around Toomer's Corner.

We beat Alabama that year. We had a freshman named Vincent Edward Jackson, but he went by "Bo." Down came the goal posts. And I suddenly found myself in the middle of Legion Field, out on the fifty yard line, jumping up and down like an idiot. Suddenly I saw a bunch of TV cameramen stampeding toward me like the Four Horsemen. I spun to flee and nearly slammed into these giant Auburn lineman charging from the other direction. I looked straight up at Coach Pat Dye on their shoulders. Then I dove sideways for daylight before these two fronts clashed and put an end to me.

That was over a quarter century ago. Today, I mail-order Auburn T-shirts in bulk each year. Even way down in Tampa, Florida, someone will react to my shirt. And you know it's real:

War Eagle.

I was asked to write the following for a collectors' limited-edition reprint of one of a friend's early novels.

Introduction

Where does one start with Randy Wayne White? Probably in that bar. It was the end of the last century. Randy was headlining some reading festival in Palm Beach, and I, with my first book barely out, was a stray speck of ink on the bottom of the program. But that was the coolest thing about having a book published: You're sent on the symposium circuit and get to meet your writing idols. Being a devotee of the Florida genre, Randy was one of my biggest inspirations, but also one of the most elusive. During that initial year, I carried around a copy of my first novel, which I had my heroes sign like a yearbook. It was nearly full. Only one autograph missing.

That particular festival had all the authors staying at the Colony Hotel. Finally, the big chance. I figured, hey, it's Randy, I'll stake out the bar. Meanwhile, there was the intimidation factor. The whole reputation thing. Randy's not as much a novelist as a Florida lifestyle in residence, a latter-day Hemingway gene-spliced with Travis McGee. Was he approachable? Would he take a swing?

The questions appeared academic as the clocked ticked past 2 a.m. in the Polo Lounge. Just about to pay my tab when suddenly, from behind, a deep voice boomed through the rafters like the shock wave of an F-16 going Mach One.

Randy had arrived.

After allowing him time to deal with numerous fans from the reading fest, I timidly approached with my autograph request. He looked at the book, and then at me like I had three heads. "I didn't write this."

"No …" I said and explained the deal, and he began reading the other names I had gathered. "That's so cool." Next thing I knew, I was at his private table. Except you're never just *with* Randy. You're coiled in the Anaconda-embrace of his expansive personality and zest for living. I couldn't have been more thrilled. How gracious, I thought. But of course he's probably super nice to everyone.

The next afternoon, the phone rings in my hotel room. Someone's on the other end like they've known me for years. "Hey, Tim. I just finished swimming a couple miles in the ocean. Let's go do something."

Just like that and ever since: total friends.

So, yes, there's the Randy reputation. But there's also the writing. Which, given his persona, might seem incongruous. Or maybe not. It's the dichotomy that's led to all those Ernest bios: How can this kind of man have this deft touch with the language, this nuance of feeling with characters and emotion. The answer is not a contradiction. It's the same ferocious hunger for other things simply applied to Randy's craft. There were always signs he would make it, this desire you could smell a mile away, like the time in the mid-70s when the classic Florida novel *92 in the Shade* by Thomas McGuane had just been made into a movie starring Peter Fonda. They were holding the premiere in Key West, and Randy went to a T-shirt shop and ordered a custom, security-staff shirt with the name of the movie -- and crashed the thing. More conventional, of course, were the early Randy Striker books that started it all, and he never looked back, soon pounding out the prolific and best-selling Doc Ford series. That's the other, lesser-known side of White, the one who sequesters himself for months, denying pleasures and friends like a monk, until his work is done. And then, and only then, does he cut loose. With the same intensity.

For whatever reason -- back at that book festival so long ago -- he immediately took me under his wing. But with Randy, it was more like being picked up hitch-hiking by Hunter Thompson. Because that's the thing about Randy: Whatever he's got planned, you always end up doing something different, and it's always a fiasco, and it's always *better*. Like the time a few of us got together drinking, and in a torturously convoluted story best saved for another day, Randy accidentally put me in this situation where I unwittingly broke up the marriage of one of his friends. In other words, your typical Randy story: We can all laugh about it *now*.

And if you're fortunate enough to be considered a close friend, there are the phone calls:

"Let's go to the bar."

"Let's go to that restaurant."

"Let's go to *Cuba*."

Then you show up at his house, and he waves and takes off wind-surfing across Pine Island Sound.

There goes my buddy Randy.

Tim Dorsey
Kissimmee, Florida
Feb. 24, 2006

Miami Book Fair, 2011

Part Seven

The Riptide Ultra-Glide

A Preview of the next Serge Storms novel, coming January 2013

Prologue
Florida

The hookers were slap-fighting a Hare Krishna up at the intersection when the bullet came through the windshield.

Until then, the tourists' rental car didn't have a mark and would have passed the damage inspection back at the airport, but this was usually hard to overlook.

It was shortly after 11 on a hot Thursday morning, and the hole in the glass was neat and small, just above the steering wheel, with a tiny circle of cracks indicating a high-velocity round. The Chevy Impala continued straight for almost a block before the horn blared from the driver's forehead. Then it veered over the center line and clipped an oncoming Nissan. Both cars spun out in opposite directions, sending other traffic screeching toward curbs and sidewalks and hookers.

Finally it was still.

Two surviving tourists in the Impala stared at each other in shock. "What just happened?"

Then it was unstill.

The driver's side windows exploded from more gunfire, this time a MAC-10 submachine gun preferred throughout the metropolitan statistical area. The tourists ducked in a spray of glass. A twelve-gauge blasted open the trunk. The pair spilled from the passenger door, onto the burning pavement, and scrambled hands and knees up the middle of U.S. Highway 1.

More bullets raked the car; others took chunks from the street around the fleeing tourists. The attack came from a black Jeep Cherokee with all the fog-light trimmings. It had skidded up sideways behind the crashed Nissan. Overloaded with passengers, an armed clown car, leathery men in cowboy hats and plaid shirts. Jumping out and firing as they advanced, as if it were completely normal behavior in south Florida. They had a point.

They were along a stretch of U.S. 1, also called Federal Highway, between Fort Lauderdale and Miami. No man's land. A gritty corridor of strip malls, service stations, old mom-and-pop motels and new bank branches.

Calls flooded 9-1-1 operators. Stray rounds shattered glass at a pizza place and nail salon.

Another vehicle arrived. A silver Ford Explorer with Kentucky plates cut the corner through a Citgo station and stopped half over the curb at a Walgreens. More men with guns. Blue jeans, T-shirts, boots. The newcomers began firing on the gunmen from the Jeep Cherokee. Two immediately got hit, MAC-10s twirling and shooting the sky as they went down. The rest ran back behind their car and returned fire on the Ford. Both groups occasionally turned to squeeze off shots at the Impala and the tourists.

A police helicopter swooped over the scene, looking down at the geometry of a Wild West corral: The Jeep on the east side of the street, the Ford on the west, and to the south, the Impala, forming a tight triangulation of fire. The tourists were on the far side of their car, desperately crawling low down the center line. The would have headed for the side of the road, but the positions of the other vehicles was placing fire along both edges of the street. The helicopter saw them and got on the radio.

The first patrol car screamed north up the middle of the highway. He saw the tourists and swung around the couple, placing his cruiser between them and the bullets. The officer jumped out and opened the back door. "Get in!"

The tourists began standing up.

A concentrated salvo from the Jeep blew out two of the patrol car's tires and most of the windows.

"Get down!"

The officer joined them on the pavement.

"What do we do?" asked the woman.

"See that copy shop?" said the officer. "We need to get around the corner."

"I feel safer here," said her husband.

The cop shook his head. "Some of those rounds are armor piercing."

The woman couldn't command her shaking legs to move. Tears. "I can't do it."

A bullet came through the door of the police car and chipped the pavement near her head. She took off like a track star, shots pocking the street around her feet. The men were right behind.

They made it around the side of the building and flattened against a wall, plaster from the storefront spraying behind them. The officer grabbed his shoulder mike to radio their position.

"What's on earth's going on?" asked the man.

"Probably find out on the news tonight," said the officer. "Do you know any of those people?"

Two heads shook. "Never seen them before."

"What about the dead driver in your car? ..."

***

A thin, wiry man in a tropical shirt stood on the second-floor balcony of one of the mom-and-pops.

A shorter, plumper man hid behind him and peeked around his side. "They're shooting down there!"

Serge smiled and continued filming with his camcorder. "I love the beach season."

"Where is the beach?"

Serge aimed an arm. "About a mile east and another world away, magnificent sand and surf, with the postcard-ready Highway A1A running along the shore. Most tourists take root out there and never get dick-deep into the underbelly. That's why I love U.S. 1!" Serge shouted the last part loud enough for one of the shooters to look up. Serge waved back. "Humid yet dusty at the same time, harsh egg-yoke tints, devoid of vegetation except the most determined wild palms fighting their way up between the pavement and concrete-blocks. And the foot traffic, a rudderless rhythm of the same bad choices and narrow appetites, trudging the streets at all hours like the undead. ... But every now and then, a fortunate tourist will confuse U.S. 1 with A1A, and accidentally book a room out here and get to dig it like a native!"

A bullet clanged off the balcony railing near the stairs.

Coleman tugged Serge's shirt. "Maybe we should go back inside."

"And miss this great footage? We're going to be famous!"

"But you're already famous, sort of," said Coleman. "All those murders. The cops call you a serial--"

"Shut up." Serge winced. "I hate that term. Serial killers are losers."

"How are you different?"

"A victim of circumstance." Serge zoomed in on the Jeep. "What are the odds all those assholes would cross my path?"

"So you're filming another documentary like the one you shot at spring break?"

"No, I've got a new hook." He panned to the Explorer. "I misjudged the market for that last project. I went for the non-market because nobody tries to reach them."

"Non-market?" asked Coleman.

"The people who never watch TV or movies, so I figured it was wide-open territory. But no takers, not even a nibble."

Another bullet hit their building two rooms down. Coleman took a swig from a pint of Jim Beam. "But I liked your spring break documentary. It had topless chicks, frat boys funneling beers and me burying my vomit in the sand."

Serge shrugged. "Documentaries are too intellectual for the general public."

"Then what's your new hook?"

"I already explained it to you, and we've been filming for over a week. Were you high?"

"Yes, tell me again."

"A reality show," said Serge. "I was surfing the channels, and you wouldn't believe the drek the cable people are putting out these days. Not even good reality. We come home at the end of the day and turn on the tube and watch the bullshit parts of what we just came in from: people cooking, working on motorcycles, trying to lose weight, getting fired, getting tattoos, getting their car repossessed, going broke and pawning World War I gas masks, suing ex-boyfriends in small claims over the power bill, couples stressed out because they had ten kids, speeders making excuses to cops, truckers driving on bad roads, guys rummaging through abandoned storage units, a dude who does a bunch of jobs that cover him with filth, a game show in a taxi, interventions for people who hoard trash, families getting their kitchens remodeled against their will."

Coleman took another slug of whiskey. "What about Cupcake Wars?"

"That one sounded promising," said Serge. "So I tuned in one night, and no fighting at all. Just a lot of frosting. What the fuck?"

"Who do you think will buy your show?"

"Probably MTV." Serge swung his camera toward more arriving police cars. "Our reality show will beat those Jersey Shore mooks like a gong. They even had the gall to set their second season on South Beach, but that was an antiseptically controlled environment. They'd never survive the real Florida. Inside a week, Snooki would be blowing winos for cigarette butts."

"I'd watch that," said Coleman.

"And that's why everyone will definitely watch our show."

"I've got the title," said Coleman. "Scumbag Shore."

Serge nodded. "I'll run it by the suits."

"The only thing I don't understand is you're just filming other people at a distance." Coleman killed the pint and fired up a jay. "If it's our reality show, aren't we supposed to be in it?"

Serge pulled a 9 millimeter pistol from under his tropical shirt and headed for the stairs.

"That's what we're going to do now."

"But they're still shooting."

"Good, I was afraid we'd get left out." Serge waved his gun vaguely at the street. "Let's go down there and interact with our peeps."

Coleman tossed the nub of his joint off the balcony and jogged to catch up. "Who are we going to interact with?"

"Thought we'd start with those two tourists who were crawling on their hands and knees through gunfire up the middle of U.S. 1." Serge racked the chamber of his pistol. "Most visitors could stay here for days without experiencing that kind of genuine Welcome-to-Florida Zeitgeist.

Since they're probably thrilled with their beginner's luck, we'll hook up and I'll take them on a behind-the-scenes tour of the sunshine state that will trip their minds. I have a hunch they won't forget this vacation."

FLA. APR. '62

Made in the USA
Charleston, SC
15 February 2013